BETTY CROCKER'S
Hamburger Cookbook

Photography Director: George Ancona

Illustrator: Barbara Bascove

GOLDEN PRESS / NEW YORK
Western Publishing Company, Inc.
Racine, Wisconsin

First Printing, 1973
Copyright © 1973 by General Mills, Inc., Minneapolis, Minnesota.
All rights reserved. Produced in the U.S.A.
Library of Congress Catalog Card Number: 73-84541

Dear Meal Planner—

Have you noticed what's been happening to hamburger? From a humble economy food, reserved for family only, it has flowered into a great American tradition.

Today hamburger can be anything the occasion calls for: a nutritious meal-in-minutes for toddlers...a noon, night or wee-hours staple for teen-agers...a swift-and-simple or gourmet-grand entrée for adults. You can serve it solo, backed only by a bun, or you can mingle it richly with vegetables, cheeses, pastas or sauces. Change its shape and you change its name. It's a meat loaf! It's a meatball! It's a superdish! Yet with all this, hamburger is still a thrift food, pound for protein-packed pound, one of the best buys on the meat market.

So this book is dedicated to bringing you up to date on hamburger in all its infinite variety, from basic recipes to fabulous flights of fancy. Have you ever tried sausage-centered burgers? Avocado-topped taco patties? Wine-marinated hamburger kabobs? Or a meat loaf filled with such exotica as bananas, green pepper and orange marmalade? No? Well...here's your chance.

And because hamburger is so eminently freezeable, we've created a collection of special "freezer mixes" and other dishes to stow away for future reference. Finally, for those of you lucky enough to have a microwave oven, we've adapted some typical recipes to use in this fascinating time-saving appliance.

We hope you'll sample liberally from the recipes on the following pages. We think they'll help you capture the spirit of hamburger as it is today.

Cordially,

Betty Crocker

P.S. All these recipes were tested in the Betty Crocker Kitchens and in the homes of hamburger-lovers all across the country. So you can be sure that they'll work for you too.

Contents

All About Hamburger

Few cuts of meat have as much going for them —or for you—as hamburger. And its number-one virtue is versatility. You can use it as the basis for a snack, sandwich or main dish. You can keep it family-frank or dress it up for company. In fact, hamburger can put on just about any face a good cook wants it to. But even a can't-go-wrong meat like this has its finer points. And once you know these few ifs, ands and buts, you'll be that much farther ahead in the cooking game.

What's in a Name?

As far as most of us are concerned, "hamburger" is just another word for ground beef. There is, however, a distinction. And it's one that you should know about when it comes to the shopping scene. Federal laws specify the amount of fat permitted in the various types of ground beef; so it is really the amount of fat (or conversely, the amount of lean*) that determines the label. Here, then, are all those names you should know about:

*Note that we express the fat-lean levels in the various types of ground beef in terms of the fat. There may be some sections of the country that use the percentage of lean instead; therefore, a 30 percent fat level would be expressed as 70 percent lean.

HAMBURGER: Any ground beef bearing this label can legally contain up to 30 percent fat. And this fat may consist of the natural fat attached to the beef plus "loose" beef fat.

GROUND BEEF: Here the amount of fat allowed under the law may also be 30 percent. The big difference between the *ground beef* and *hamburger* labels is that *ground beef* can contain *only* the fat attached to the beef. No other fat may be added to reach the 30 percent level. Thus, the fat content in meat labeled *ground beef* is usually less than 30 percent.

LEAN GROUND BEEF (GROUND CHUCK): The fat level in ground beef bearing this label is usually about 20 percent.

EXTRA LEAN GROUND BEEF (GROUND ROUND): This type of ground beef usually contains about 15 percent fat.

Keep an eye out too for ground beef supplemented with vegetable protein sources—it's now available in some parts of the country. The labels for this type of beef mixture vary, but it is usually an excellent bargain.

Most of the recipes in this book were tested with *ground beef*—except for a few that call for a leaner cut, and they so specify.

Which One's for You?

It all depends. On your recipe and your budget. For a juicy broiled or grilled burger, your choice should be *ground beef* or *ground chuck*. The amount of fat in both types allows the burgers to baste themselves. If you prefer a leaner type, you will probably have a less juicy patty. But remember, the more fat, the more shrinkage.

Ground round and *ground chuck* are ideal for casseroles and other main dishes, though the fattier cuts will work just as well if you can drain off the excess fat after the meat has been browned.

And then there's the cost. The more fat, the lower the cost—that only stands to reason. Demand is another factor that affects the price tag. *Ground round* and *ground chuck* are more expensive because of all the other (and more costly) uses the butcher has for them. So here you must pay for your preferences.

No matter which label you head for, all types of ground beef should have a nice bright color. Fresh ground beef crumbles easily and smells good; a slick feel and an "off" odor are signs of age.

How to Store

Ground beef is far more perishable than other beef cuts. The grinding, quite naturally, exposes more of the meat to the air—hence, to bacteria. Therefore, a certain amount of care is called for.

If you're planning to use ground beef *within* 24 hours of purchase, you can store it in the meat keeper or the coldest part of your refrigerator. Prepackaged ground beef should be refrigerated right in its package, unopened. Beef ground to order, however, should be rewrapped loosely in waxed paper or aluminum foil and then refrigerated.

If you plan to store the ground beef for a while —and that means longer than 24 hours—then freeze you must. To maintain the meat's quality, first wrap it in an airtight, moisture-proof wrap. If burgers are part of your future plans, you can shape the meat into patties and stack them with a double layer of foil or freezer wrap between; then overwrap. Do not freeze ground beef longer than 3 to 4 months.

It's best to thaw ground beef still in its wrap in the refrigerator. If time is tight, you can use your microwave oven for speedy thawing (follow the manufacturer's instructions), or you can cook it from the frozen state—providing no handling is necessary and no additions are to be made before the meat is browned.

SEASON-UPS

Below you will find a list of herbs and spices that are all compatible with hamburger. Start with a small amount and increase until you find the just-right flavor level.

allspice	curry powder	oregano
basil	garlic	paprika
cayenne red pepper	ginger	parsley
celery seed	mace	sage
chili powder	marjoram	savory
cumin seed	mustard	sesame seed
	nutmeg	thyme

Patties & Sandwiches

Basic Hamburgers

1½ pounds ground beef
1 small onion, finely chopped (about ¼ cup)
¼ cup water or evaporated milk
1 teaspoon salt
1 teaspoon Worcestershire sauce
¼ teaspoon pepper

Mix all ingredients. Shape mixture into 6 patties, about ¾ inch thick. Broil or grill patties 4 inches from heat, turning once, to desired doneness, 10 to 15 minutes. Nice served on toasted buns with favorite topping.

6 patties.

VARIATIONS

Before mixing ingredients, add one or more of the following:

1 tablespoon horseradish
1 tablespoon prepared mustard
1 tablespoon snipped chives
1 to 2 tablespoons crumbled blue cheese
2 tablespoons sesame seed
¼ cup chopped ripe olives
¼ cup chopped dill pickle or pickle relish
¼ cup chopped nuts

Have a freezer? See page 70 for Freezer Burgers.

Hamburger Toppings

BROILED ONION TOPPING

1 tablespoon butter or margarine
2 medium onions, chopped (about 1 cup)
⅛ teaspoon nutmeg
2 tablespoons dairy sour cream

Melt butter in small skillet. Add onions; cook and stir until tender. Stir in remaining ingredients; spread on cooked patties. Broil 2 inches from heat until hot, about 1 minute.

Enough for 6 patties.

MUSHROOM-ONION TOPPER

1 tablespoon butter or margarine
1 medium onion, thinly sliced
1 can (4 ounces) mushroom stems and
   pieces, drained
½ teaspoon Worcestershire sauce
⅛ teaspoon pepper

Melt butter in small skillet. Add onion; cook and stir until tender. Stir in remaining ingredients and heat. Serve hot over patties.

Enough for 6 patties.

MUSTARD BUTTER

¼ cup butter or margarine, softened
1 tablespoon snipped parsley
2 tablespoons prepared mustard
¼ teaspoon onion salt

Mix all ingredients. Spoon onto hot patties.

Enough for 6 patties.

SESAME BUTTER

¼ cup butter or margarine, softened
1 teaspoon Worcestershire sauce
½ teaspoon garlic salt
1 tablespoon toasted sesame seed (see note)

Mix all ingredients. Spoon onto hot patties.

Enough for 4 patties.

NOTE: To toast sesame seed, spread in ungreased shallow baking pan and bake in 350° oven until golden brown, 5 to 10 minutes.

ZIPPY TOMATO SAUCE

2 tablespoons butter or margarine
½ cup chopped green pepper
1 small onion, thinly sliced
1 can (8 ounces) tomato sauce
1 cup chili sauce
1 teaspoon Worcestershire sauce
¼ teaspoon chili powder

Melt butter in small saucepan. Add green pepper and onion; cook and stir until onion is tender. Stir in remaining ingredients. Heat to boiling, stirring occasionally. Serve hot over patties.

Enough for 8 patties.

FILLED HAMBURGERS

1½ pounds ground beef
¼ cup dry bread crumbs
1 small onion, finely chopped (about
   ¼ cup)
1 egg
1 teaspoon salt
1 teaspoon Worcestershire sauce
¼ teaspoon pepper
   Fillings (below)

Mix all ingredients except fillings. Shape mixture into 12 thin patties, about 3½ inches in diameter. Top each of 6 patties with a filling, spreading to within ½ inch of edge. Cover with a remaining patty, sealing edges firmly. Broil or grill patties 4 inches from heat, turning once, to desired doneness, about 10 minutes.

6 patties.

MIX-AND-MATCH FILLINGS

Use one or more of the following:

Dill pickle slices or pickle relish
Prepared mustard
Catsup
Horseradish
Onion slices or finely chopped onion
Tomato slices
Process American or Cheddar cheese slices

PEPPY CHEESE FILLING

½ cup shredded process American or
   Cheddar cheese
2 tablespoons mayonnaise or salad dressing
1 teaspoon Worcestershire sauce
½ teaspoon salt
½ teaspoon prepared mustard
¼ teaspoon pepper

Mix all ingredients.

KEEP THE SECRET

If you fill a burger, don't spoil the surprise inside. Be sure to keep the filling in the center of the patty and press the outer edges together firmly. The egg and bread crumbs in the Filled Hamburgers recipe keep the patties moist—no danger of pulling apart as they cook. What's inside remains a secret.

NIFTY HAMBURGERS ON A BUN

8 small hamburger buns, split, or 6 slices
   bread
   Prepared mustard or catsup
1 pound lean ground beef (chuck)
1 small onion, chopped (about ¼ cup)
1 teaspoon salt
¼ teaspoon pepper

Heat oven to 500°. Spread cut sides of hamburger buns or one side of each bread slice with mustard. Mix meat, onion, salt and pepper. Spread mixture over mustard, being careful to bring it to edges of buns. Place meat sides up on ungreased baking sheet. Bake until of desired doneness, about 5 minutes.

4 to 6 servings.

NOTE: If you like, you can have these burgers ready and waiting in the freezer for last-minute cooking. After spreading meat mixture over buns, wrap each securely in heavy-duty or double thickness regular aluminum foil and label; freeze no longer than 2 months. To serve, unwrap desired number of hamburgers and bake about 10 minutes.

FAMILY FAVORITE BURGERS

1½ pounds ground beef
 2 slices bread, torn into small pieces
 ⅓ cup milk
 ¼ cup catsup
 1 small onion, finely chopped (about
    ¼ cup)
 1 teaspoon salt
 2 teaspoons horseradish
 2 teaspoons Worcestershire sauce
 1 tablespoon prepared mustard

Mix all ingredients. Shape mixture into 6 patties, about ¾ inch thick. Broil or grill patties 4 inches from heat, turning once, to desired doneness, 10 to 15 minutes.

6 patties.

ZESTY BURGERS

 1 pound ground beef
 ⅓ cup dry bread crumbs
 ½ cup water
 1 teaspoon instant beef bouillon
 1 teaspoon grated lemon peel
 1 teaspoon lemon juice
 ½ teaspoon salt
 ½ teaspoon sage
 ½ teaspoon ginger
 ¼ teaspoon pepper

Mix all ingredients. Shape mixture into 4 patties, about ¾ inch thick. Broil or grill patties 4 inches from heat, turning once, to desired doneness, 10 to 15 minutes.

4 patties.

BURGUNDY BURGERS

1½ pounds ground beef
 ¼ cup Burgundy or other red wine
 1 small onion, finely chopped (about
    ¼ cup)
 1 tablespoon Worcestershire sauce
 1 teaspoon seasoned salt
 ¼ teaspoon pepper
 ⅛ teaspoon garlic salt

Mix all ingredients. Shape mixture into 6 patties, about ¾ inch thick. Broil or grill patties 4 inches from heat, turning once, to desired doneness, 10 to 15 minutes. Nice served on toasted buns with a favorite topping (see page 7).

6 patties.

VARIATION

Blue Cheese Burgundy Burgers: Shape meat mixture into 12 thin patties, about 3½ inches in diameter. Place 1 tablespoon crumbled blue cheese on each of 6 patties. Top with a remaining patty, sealing edges firmly.

SUPREME BURGERS

 2 pounds ground beef
 1 envelope (about 1½ ounces) onion soup
    mix
 ½ cup dry bread crumbs
 1 cup dairy sour cream
 ⅛ teaspoon pepper

Mix all ingredients. Shape mixture into 8 patties, about ¾ inch thick. Broil or grill patties 4 inches from heat, turning once, to desired doneness, 10 to 15 minutes.

8 patties.

BLUE RIBBON BURGERS

2 pounds ground beef
2 teaspoons Worcestershire sauce
½ teaspoon salt
¼ teaspoon garlic salt
¼ teaspoon pepper
1 package (3 ounces) cream cheese, softened
2 tablespoons crumbled blue cheese
1 can (4 ounces) mushroom stems and
  pieces, drained and chopped

Mix meat, Worcestershire sauce and seasonings. Shape mixture into 12 thin patties, about 4 inches in diameter.

Mix cream cheese and blue cheese. Top each of 6 patties with cheese mixture, spreading to within ½ inch of edge; press mushrooms into cheese. Cover each with a remaining patty, sealing edges firmly. Broil or grill patties 4 inches from heat, turning once, to desired doneness, 10 to 15 minutes. (Pictured on the cover.)

6 large patties.

BRAUNBURGERS

1 pound ground beef
¼ pound Braunschweiger (liver) sausage
¼ cup dairy sour cream
2 tablespoons finely chopped onion

Mix all ingredients. Shape mixture into 5 patties, about ¾ inch thick. Broil or grill patties 4 inches from heat, turning once, to desired doneness, 10 to 15 minutes.

5 patties.

NOTE: Because of the zesty sausage, no additional seasonings are necessary.

BEEF BOULETTE BURGERS

2 pounds ground beef
1 cup dairy sour cream
½ cup dry bread crumbs
1 can (4 ounces) mushroom stems and
  pieces, drained and chopped
2 tablespoons finely chopped onion
2 tablespoons snipped parsley
1½ teaspoons salt
¼ teaspoon pepper

Mix all ingredients. Shape mixture into 8 patties, about ¾ inch thick. Broil or grill patties 4 inches from heat, turning once, to desired doneness, 10 to 15 minutes. (Pictured on page 24.)

8 patties.

CRUNCHY TERIYAKI BURGERS

1½ pounds ground beef
½ cup finely chopped water chestnuts
¼ cup soy sauce
¼ cup dry sherry or orange juice
1 clove garlic, minced
1 teaspoon molasses or brown sugar
⅛ teaspoon ginger

Mix meat and water chestnuts. Shape mixture into 6 patties, about ¾ inch thick. Place patties in ungreased baking dish, 10×6×1¾ inches. Mix remaining ingredients; pour over patties. Cover and refrigerate at least 3 hours, turning patties once.

Remove patties from marinade. Broil or grill patties 4 inches from heat to desired doneness, 10 to 15 minutes. Brush frequently with marinade and turn once.

6 patties.

CHILI CHEESE BURGERS

1½ pounds ground beef
1 small onion, finely chopped (about
    ¼ cup)
1 teaspoon chili powder
1 teaspoon Worcestershire sauce
¾ teaspoon salt
¼ teaspoon garlic salt
¼ teaspoon pepper
¼ teaspoon red pepper sauce
    Dash cayenne red pepper
6 slices Cheddar cheese, 2 × 2 inches
2 tablespoons canned chopped green
    chilies

Mix all ingredients except cheese and chilies. Shape mixture into 12 thin patties, about 3½ inches in diameter. Place 1 cheese slice and 1 teaspoon chilies on each of 6 patties. Top with a remaining patty, sealing edges firmly. Broil or grill patties 4 inches from heat, turning once, to desired doneness, 10 to 15 minutes. (Pictured on page 24.)

6 patties.

CARAWAY BURGERS

1½ pounds ground beef
1 medium onion, finely chopped (about
    ½ cup)
1 teaspoon salt
1 teaspoon caraway seed
1 teaspoon Worcestershire sauce
¼ teaspoon pepper
1 cup beer

Mix all ingredients except beer. Shape mixture into 6 patties, about 1 inch thick. Place in ungreased baking dish, 10 × 6 × 1¾ inches. Pour beer over patties; cover and refrigerate at least 3 hours (the meat may turn gray).

Remove patties from marinade. Broil or grill patties 4 inches from heat, turning once, to desired doneness, 15 to 20 minutes.

6 patties.

NOTE: If you prefer to make thinner patties, use a larger dish for marinating and turn patties occasionally while marinating. Broil or grill 10 to 15 minutes.

REUBEN BURGERS

1 pound ground beef
1 can (4½ ounces) corned beef spread
    or deviled ham
1 small onion, finely chopped (about
    ¼ cup)
¼ teaspoon salt
⅛ teaspoon garlic salt
⅛ teaspoon pepper
1 can (8 ounces) sauerkraut, drained
5 slices Swiss cheese, 3 × 3 inches

Mix all ingredients except sauerkraut and cheese. Shape mixture into 5 patties, about ¾ inch thick.

Set oven control at broil and/or 550°. Broil patties 4 inches from heat, turning once, to desired doneness, 10 to 15 minutes. Top each patty with sauerkraut and a cheese slice. Broil until cheese is light brown.

Nice served on toasted rye or pumpernickel buns. (Pictured on page 25.)

5 patties.

A TIGHT FIT?

Ever found yourself in a skillet squeeze? Sometimes it just isn't possible to brown all the patties evenly in one step. So brown half at a time. Once browned, return all to the skillet (they shrink a bit and help the fit), add the sauce or other ingredients and go along as directed. Fancy footwork to two-step success.

TACO PATTIES

1½ pounds ground beef
1 small onion, chopped (about ¼ cup)
1 teaspoon salt
1 teaspoon Worcestershire sauce
¼ teaspoon pepper
¾ cup water
1 envelope (about 1¼ ounces) taco seasoning mix
1 ripe small avocado*
1 cup shredded Cheddar cheese (4 ounces)

Mix meat, onion, salt, Worcestershire sauce and pepper. Shape mixture into 6 patties, about ¾ inch thick. Brown patties in large skillet over medium-high heat, turning once. Remove patties and set aside. Pour fat from skillet.

Mix water and seasoning mix in same skillet; heat to boiling, stirring constantly. Reduce heat; return patties to skillet and turn each to coat with sauce.

Peel avocado and cut into 6 rings. Top each patty with an avocado ring; cover and simmer 10 minutes. Sprinkle with cheese; cover and heat until cheese is melted, about 2 minutes. Serve sauce over patties. (Pictured on page 24.)

Serve with refried beans and corn chips for a Mexicali meal.

6 patties.

* You can substitute 1 medium tomato, sliced, for the avocado rings.

DEVILISH POTATO STACKS

1 pound ground beef
1 can (2¼ ounces) deviled ham
1 teaspoon Worcestershire sauce
  Instant mashed potato puffs
  (enough for 4 servings)
½ cup creamed cottage cheese
1 can (3½ ounces) French fried onions

Heat oven to 350°. Mix meat, deviled ham and Worcestershire sauce. Shape mixture into 4 patties. Place patties in ungreased baking pan, 8 × 8 × 2 inches.

Prepare potato puffs as directed on package except—decrease water to 1 cup. Stir cottage cheese and half the onions into potatoes. Top each patty with ¼ of the potato mixture. Sprinkle with remaining onions. Bake uncovered to desired doneness, 30 to 40 minutes. Remove patties to serving plate with a slotted spoon.

4 patties.

TRIPLE CHEESE PATTIES

1½ pounds ground beef
¼ cup dry bread crumbs
1 small onion, chopped (about ¼ cup)
1 egg
1 teaspoon salt
1 teaspoon Worcestershire sauce
½ teaspoon basil leaves
¼ teaspoon pepper
⅛ teaspoon garlic salt
6 tablespoons creamed cottage cheese
¼ cup grated Parmesan cheese
1 can (8 ounces) tomato sauce
6 slices mozzarella or Swiss cheese,
3 × 3 inches

Mix meat, bread crumbs, onion, egg and seasonings. Shape mixture into 12 thin patties, about 4 inches in diameter.

Top each of 6 patties with 1 tablespoon cottage cheese, spreading to within ½ inch of edge; sprinkle with 2 teaspoons Parmesan cheese. Cover each with a remaining patty, sealing edges firmly.

Brown patties in large skillet over medium-high heat, turning once. Drain off fat. Pour tomato sauce over patties; cover and simmer 15 minutes. Place a cheese slice on each patty; cover and heat until cheese is melted, about 2 minutes. Serve sauce over patties. (Pictured on page 25.)

6 patties.

HAMBURGERS AU POIVRE

1 pound ground beef
½ teaspoon salt
½ to 1 tablespoon freshly cracked black
pepper
1 tablespoon cognac or brandy (optional)
3 tablespoons dry red wine (optional)

Mix meat and salt. Shape mixture into 4 patties, about ¾ inch thick. Press pepper into both sides of each patty. Cook patties in large skillet over medium-high heat, turning once, to desired doneness, about 8 minutes. Drain off fat.

Sprinkle cognac over patties; immediately ignite if desired. Remove patties to warm platter.

Stir wine into drippings in skillet; heat just to boiling, stirring constantly. Serve sauce over patties.

4 patties.

PATTIES PARMIGIANA

1½ pounds ground beef (see note)
1 small onion, finely chopped (about
   ¼ cup)
1 teaspoon salt
1 teaspoon Worcestershire sauce
¼ teaspoon pepper
½ cup grated Parmesan cheese
¼ cup cornflake crumbs
1 egg, slightly beaten
1 can (8 ounces) tomato sauce
1 teaspoon Italian seasoning
6 slices mozzarella cheese, 3 × 3 inches

Mix meat, onion, salt, Worcestershire sauce and pepper. Shape mixture into 6 patties, about ¾ inch thick. Mix Parmesan cheese and cornflake crumbs. Dip patties into egg, then coat with crumb mixture. Brown patties in large skillet over medium heat, turning once. Drain off fat.

Mix tomato sauce and Italian seasoning; pour over patties in skillet. Cover and simmer 15 minutes. Top each patty with a cheese slice; cover and heat until cheese is melted, about 2 minutes. Serve sauce over patties.

6 patties.

NOTE: If ground beef is lean, it may be necessary to add a small amount of shortening or salad oil to the skillet when browning patties.

A FUTURE INVESTMENT

Take advantage of the fact that hamburger patties adapt nicely to do-ahead shaping. In fact, the waiting time in the refrigerator gives the seasonings a better chance to mingle with the meat, actually improving the taste. Try it someday soon. You'll be ahead on time and up on flavor.

HAMBURGERS DIANE

2 tablespoons butter or margarine
1 teaspoon Worcestershire sauce
¼ teaspoon lemon juice
1 clove garlic, minced
1 small onion, sliced
1 cup washed, trimmed sliced mushrooms*
1 pound lean ground beef (chuck)
½ teaspoon salt
¼ teaspoon pepper

Melt butter in large skillet. Add Worcestershire sauce, lemon juice, garlic, onion and mushrooms; cook and stir over medium heat 2 minutes. Remove from heat.

Mix meat, salt and pepper. Shape mixture into 4 patties, about ¾ inch thick. Push mushroom-onion mixture to side of skillet. Cook patties in same skillet over medium-high heat, turning once, to desired doneness, about 10 minutes. Serve mushroom-onion mixture over patties. (Pictured on page 25.)

4 patties.

* You can substitute ½ cup drained canned sliced mushrooms for the fresh mushrooms.

BARBECUE HAMBURGER PATTIES

1½ pounds ground beef
  1 medium onion, chopped (about ½ cup)
  1 teaspoon salt
  ⅓ cup catsup
  ⅓ cup chili sauce
  2 tablespoons brown sugar
  1 tablespoon lemon juice

Mix meat, onion and salt. Shape mixture into 6 patties, about ¾ inch thick. Brown patties in large skillet over medium-high heat, turning once. Cover and cook over low heat 10 minutes. Drain off fat.

Mix catsup, chili sauce, brown sugar and lemon juice; pour over patties. Cover and simmer 15 minutes, spooning sauce onto patties occasionally. Serve sauce over patties.

6 patties.

BAVARIAN PATTIES WITH SAUERKRAUT

1½ pounds ground beef
  ½ cup applesauce
  ⅓ cup dry bread crumbs
  1 small onion, finely chopped (about
    ¼ cup)
  1 egg
  1 teaspoon salt
  ½ teaspoon allspice
  1 can (16 ounces) sauerkraut, drained

Mix all ingredients except sauerkraut. Shape mixture into 6 patties, about ¾ inch thick. Brown patties in large skillet over medium heat, turning once. Drain off fat. Spoon sauerkraut onto patties; cover and simmer 15 minutes.

6 patties.

SAUSAGE-CENTERED HAMBURGER ROLLS

1½ pounds ground beef
  1 cup finely chopped unpared apple
  ⅓ cup chopped green onion (with tops)
  1 egg
  1 teaspoon salt
  ¼ teaspoon pepper
  ¼ teaspoon cinnamon
    Dash cloves
  1 package (8 ounces) brown and serve
    sausage links
  2 tablespoons flour
  1 teaspoon instant beef bouillon
  1 cup water

Mix meat, apple, onion, egg and seasonings. Divide mixture into 10 equal parts. Mold each part around a sausage link, sealing ends. Brown meat rolls in large skillet over medium heat. Remove meat rolls.

Pour all but 2 tablespoons fat from skillet. Stir flour into fat remaining in skillet. Cook over low heat, stirring constantly, until mixture is smooth and bubbly. Stir in bouillon and water. Heat to boiling, stirring constantly. Reduce heat; return meat rolls to skillet. Cover and simmer 15 minutes.

Buttered noodles are a good "go-with" for this zesty dish.

6 to 8 servings.

BEEF AND CABBAGE JOES

1 pound ground beef
1 medium onion, chopped (about ½ cup)
½ cup thinly sliced celery
2 cups shredded cabbage
⅓ cup chopped green pepper
¾ cup catsup
¼ cup water
¼ teaspoon salt
1 tablespoon prepared mustard
8 hamburger buns, split and toasted

Cook and stir meat, onion and celery in large skillet until meat is brown. Drain off fat. Stir in cabbage, green pepper, catsup, water, salt and mustard: heat to boiling, stirring occasionally. Reduce heat; cover and simmer until vegetables are tender, about 25 minutes. Spoon mixture onto bottom halves of buns; top with remaining halves.

8 sandwiches.

NOTE: If you have a microwave oven, see page 74 for specific instructions.

VARIATION

Sloppy Joes: Omit cabbage and salt.

CHOW MEIN ON A BUN

1 pound ground beef
1 medium onion, thinly sliced
⅔ cup water
2 tablespoons cornstarch
3 tablespoons soy sauce
1 tablespoon molasses
¼ teaspoon ginger
1 can (16 ounces) bean sprouts, rinsed
   and drained
1 can (8½ ounces) water chestnuts, drained
   and sliced
8 hamburger buns, split and toasted

Cook and stir meat and onion in large skillet until onion is tender. Drain off fat. Mix water, cornstarch, soy sauce, molasses and ginger; stir into meat mixture. Add bean sprouts and water chestnuts. Cook, stirring constantly, until mixture thickens and boils, about 5 minutes. Serve on buns and pass additional soy sauce. (Pictured on page 25.)

8 sandwiches.

VARIATION

Chow Mein: Omit buns. Serve the chow mein mixture over hot cooked rice or chow mein noodles.

HAMBURGER PASTIES

1 pound ground beef
1 small onion, chopped (about ¼ cup)
1 can (8 ounces) peas or diced carrots, drained*
1 medium potato, pared and shredded
1 cup shredded process American or Cheddar cheese (4 ounces)
¼ cup catsup
½ teaspoon garlic salt
¼ teaspoon pepper
1 tablespoon prepared mustard
1 package (11 ounces) pie crust mix or sticks

Heat oven to 375°. Cook and stir meat and onion in large skillet until meat is brown. Drain off fat. Remove from heat; stir in remaining ingredients except pie crust mix and set aside.

Prepare pastry for Two-crust Pie as directed on package. Divide dough into 8 equal parts. Roll each part on floured surface into a 7-inch circle. On half of each circle, spread about ½ cup meat mixture (packed) to within ½ inch of edge. Moisten edge of pastry with water. Fold pastry over filling, sealing edges with fork. Place on ungreased baking sheet; prick tops with fork.

Bake 30 to 35 minutes You can serve these as sandwiches or, if you prefer, place on plates and top with a favorite gravy or sauce.

8 pasties.

* You can substitute 1 cup of a favorite cooked vegetable for the canned peas or carrots.

Like to plan ahead? See page 71 for Freezer Pasties. Or get a head start with Browned 'n Seasoned Freezer Mix (see page 63).

TACOS

MEAT FILLING

1 pound ground beef
1 medium onion, chopped (about ½ cup)
1 can (15 ounces) tomato sauce
1 teaspoon garlic salt
½ to 1 teaspoon chili powder
    Dash pepper

SHELLS AND TOPPINGS

8 to 10 taco shells
1 cup shredded Cheddar cheese (4 ounces)
1 cup shredded lettuce
1 large tomato, chopped

Cook and stir meat and onion in skillet until meat is brown. Drain off fat. Stir in tomato sauce, garlic salt, chili powder and pepper; simmer uncovered 15 minutes.

While Meat Filling is simmering, heat taco shells as directed on package. Spoon Meat Filling into taco shells. Top filling with cheese, lettuce and tomato. If desired, serve with taco sauce.

8 to 10 tacos.

You can get a head start on this recipe with Beef-Tomato Freezer Mix (see page 67).

Meatballs

Basic Meatballs

1 pound ground beef
1 egg
1 small onion, chopped (about ¼ cup)
⅓ cup dry bread crumbs
¼ cup milk
¾ teaspoon salt
⅛ teaspoon pepper
1 teaspoon Worcestershire sauce

Mix all ingredients. Shape mixture by tablespoonfuls into 1½-inch balls. (For ease in shaping meatballs, occasionally wet hands with cold water.)

TO COOK IN SKILLET: Heat 1 tablespoon salad oil in large skillet; cook meatballs over medium heat until brown, about 20 minutes. Drain off fat.

TO COOK IN OVEN: Place meatballs in lightly greased baking pan, 13×9×2 or 15½× 10½×1 inch; bake uncovered in 400° oven until light brown, about 20 minutes. Drain off fat.

About 24 meatballs.

NOTE: If you have a microwave oven, see page 73 for specific instructions.

Have a freezer? See page 71 for Freezer Meatballs.

SAUCY MEATBALLS

Basic Meatballs (page 18)
1 can (10¾ ounces) condensed cream of chicken soup
⅓ cup milk
⅛ teaspoon nutmeg
½ cup dairy sour cream
Snipped parsley

Prepare Basic Meatballs. Combine cooked meatballs, soup, milk and nutmeg in large skillet; heat to boiling, stirring occasionally. Reduce heat; cover and simmer 15 minutes. Stir in sour cream; cover and heat 2 to 3 minutes. Sprinkle with parsley. (Pictured on page 26.)

4 or 5 servings.

NOTE: If you have a microwave oven, see page 73 for specific instructions.

SWEET-AND-SOUR MEATBALLS

Basic Meatballs (page 18)
1 tablespoon cornstarch
½ cup brown sugar (packed)
1 can (13¼ ounces) pineapple tidbits
1 tablespoon soy sauce
⅓ cup vinegar
½ cup coarsely chopped green pepper

Prepare Basic Meatballs and set aside. Mix cornstarch and sugar in large skillet. Stir in pineapple (with syrup), soy sauce and vinegar. Cook, stirring constantly, until mixture thickens and boils. Add cooked meatballs; cover and simmer 10 minutes, stirring occasionally. Stir in green pepper; cover and simmer until pepper is crisp-tender, about 5 minutes.

4 or 5 servings.

PEPPER BEEF BALLS

Basic Meatballs (page 18)
1 tablespoon butter or margarine
1 medium onion, sliced
1½ cups water
1½ teaspoons instant beef bouillon
½ teaspoon garlic salt
½ teaspoon ginger
3 tablespoons soy sauce
2 medium green peppers, cut into strips
2 tablespoons cornstarch
2 tablespoons water
1 large tomato, cut into eighths

Prepare Basic Meatballs and set aside. Melt butter in large skillet. Add onion; cook and stir until tender. Add cooked meatballs, 1½ cups water, the bouillon, garlic salt, ginger and soy sauce; heat to boiling. Reduce heat; cover and simmer 10 minutes, stirring occasionally.

Add green pepper. Mix cornstarch and 2 tablespoons water; stir into sauce mixture. Cook, stirring carefully, until mixture thickens and boils. Cover and simmer until pepper is crisp-tender, about 3 minutes. Add tomato; cover and heat 2 to 3 minutes.

Hot cooked rice makes an ideal accompaniment for this zesty dish.

4 or 5 servings.

HARVEST-TIME MEATBALLS

Basic Meatballs (page 18)
2 tablespoons butter or margarine
⅛ teaspoon instant minced garlic*
½ teaspoon thyme leaves
½ pound mushrooms, washed, trimmed
   and sliced
3 medium zucchini, thinly sliced (about
   4 cups)
½ teaspoon salt
⅓ cup grated Parmesan cheese
2 tomatoes, cut into eighths

Prepare Basic Meatballs and set aside. Melt butter in large skillet. Add garlic, thyme leaves, mushrooms and zucchini; cook over medium-high heat 5 minutes, stirring occasionally.

Add cooked meatballs; cover and simmer, stirring occasionally, until vegetables are tender, about 10 minutes. Sprinkle with salt and cheese. Add tomatoes; cover and heat 2 to 3 minutes. (Pictured on page 26.)

4 or 5 servings.

* You can substitute 1 clove garlic, minced, or ⅛ teaspoon garlic powder for the instant minced garlic.

HUNGARIAN MEATBALLS

Basic Meatballs (page 18)
1 tablespoon salad oil
2 medium onions, thinly sliced
¾ cup water
¾ cup dry red wine*
1 teaspoon caraway seed
2 teaspoons paprika
½ teaspoon marjoram leaves
½ teaspoon salt
¼ cup water
2 tablespoons flour

Prepare Basic Meatballs and set aside. Heat oil in large skillet. Add onions; cook and stir until tender. Add cooked meatballs, ¾ cup water, the wine, caraway seed, paprika, marjoram leaves and salt; heat to boiling. Reduce heat; cover and simmer 30 minutes, stirring occasionally.

Mix ¼ cup water and the flour; stir into sauce mixture. Heat to boiling, stirring carefully. Boil and stir 1 minute.

Nice served with boiled potatoes or noodles.

4 or 5 servings.

* You can substitute a mixture of ¾ cup water, 1 teaspoon instant beef bouillon and 1 tablespoon vinegar for the wine.

THICKEN THIN

Juices too juicy for your taste? A simple stir-in does the customizing. Figure on using 1 to 2 tablespoons flour for each cup of liquidy liquid. But to insure a smooth saucing, *first* mix the flour with about ¼ cup water. Stir into the liquid and heat to boiling, stirring constantly. Boil and stir 1 minute. Still too thin? Do it again.

MEATBALL STEW

Basic Meatballs (page 18)
4 medium carrots, cut into 1-inch
   pieces*
2 stalks celery, cut into 1-inch pieces*
3 medium potatoes, pared and cut
   into 1-inch cubes*
1 can (16 ounces) stewed tomatoes
1 teaspoon salt
1 teaspoon instant beef bouillon
⅛ teaspoon pepper
1 bay leaf
¾ cup water

Prepare Basic Meatballs except—cook in Dutch oven. Drain off fat.

Add remaining ingredients; heat to boiling. Reduce heat; cover and simmer, stirring occasionally, until vegetables are tender, about 40 minutes. Remove bay leaf.

4 or 5 servings.

* You can substitute 1 package (24 ounces) frozen vegetables for stew for the carrots, celery and potatoes.

MEATBALL STEW WITH DUMPLINGS

Basic Meatballs (page 18)
1 can (10¾ ounces) condensed cream of
   celery soup
¼ cup dairy sour cream
1 can (16 ounces) peas, cut green beans
   or sliced carrots
1 can (15 ounces) potatoes, drained
   and sliced
   Egg Dumplings (below) or Parsley
   Dumplings (below)

Prepare Basic Meatballs except—cook meatballs in Dutch oven. Drain off fat. Add soup, sour cream, peas (with liquid) and potatoes; heat to boiling, stirring occasionally.

Prepare dumplings; drop dough by tablespoonfuls onto boiling mixture. Simmer uncovered 10 minutes. Cover and simmer 10 minutes longer.

4 or 5 servings.

EGG DUMPLINGS
2 cups biscuit baking mix
2 eggs
2 tablespoons milk

Mix all ingredients until a soft dough forms.

PARSLEY DUMPLINGS
2 cups biscuit baking mix
2 tablespoons parsley flakes
⅔ cup milk

Mix all ingredients until a soft dough forms.

PORCUPINES

1 pound ground beef
½ cup uncooked regular rice
½ cup water
1 small onion, chopped (about ¼ cup)
1 teaspoon salt
½ teaspoon celery salt
⅛ teaspoon garlic powder
⅛ teaspoon pepper
1 can (15 ounces) tomato sauce
1 cup water
2 teaspoons Worcestershire sauce

Mix meat, rice, ½ cup water, the onion and seasonings. Shape mixture by tablespoonfuls into 1½-inch balls.

TO COOK IN SKILLET: Heat 1 tablespoon salad oil in large skillet; cook meatballs over medium heat until brown. Add remaining ingredients; heat to boiling. Reduce heat; cover and simmer 45 minutes.

TO COOK IN OVEN: Place meatballs in ungreased baking dish, 8×8×2 inches. Mix remaining ingredients and pour over meatballs. Cover and bake in 350° oven 45 minutes. Uncover and bake 15 minutes longer.

4 or 5 servings.

SAUERBRATEN MEATBALLS

Basic Meatballs (page 18)
1 tablespoon brown sugar
1 teaspoon instant beef bouillon
¼ teaspoon ground cloves
⅛ teaspoon pepper
1 bay leaf
¼ cup vinegar
1½ cups water
⅓ cup raisins (optional)
6 gingersnaps, broken into pieces

Prepare Basic Meatballs. Combine cooked meatballs and remaining ingredients in large skillet; heat to boiling, stirring occasionally. Reduce heat; cover and simmer 20 minutes, stirring occasionally. Remove bay leaf.

Nice served with mashed potatoes.

4 or 5 servings.

FOCUS ON FOOD

At right—Meat loaves to fit the fancy of any family. Clockwise from upper left: Meat-and-Potato Squares (page 31), Savory Stuffed Meat Loaf (page 33), Bacon-wrapped Little Loaves (page 35), Onion Meat Loaf (page 32).

On pages 24–25—Patties either burger-style or fancy-fashion. Top row: Beef Boulette Burgers (page 10), Chili Cheese Burgers (page 11), Chow Mein on a Bun (page 16), Reuben Burgers (page 11). Bottom row: Taco Patties (page 12), Triple Cheese Patties (page 13), Hamburgers Diane (page 14).

WINE-MARINATED KABOBS

1 pound ground beef
½ pound large mushrooms, washed and
   trimmed
¼ cup salad oil
½ cup Burgundy or other red wine
1 teaspoon marjoram leaves
½ teaspoon salt
⅛ teaspoon instant minced garlic
1 teaspoon Worcestershire sauce
2 tablespoons catsup

Shape meat by tablespoonfuls into 24 balls. Place in glass bowl or plastic bag; add mushrooms. Mix remaining ingredients; pour over meatballs and mushrooms. Cover and refrigerate at least 8 hours, turning meatballs and mushrooms occasionally.

On each of four 12-inch metal skewers, alternate 6 meatballs with mushrooms.

Set oven control at broil and/or 550°. Broil kabobs 4 inches from heat to desired doneness, 15 to 20 minutes. Brush occasionally with remaining marinade and gently push with fork to turn.

4 servings.

FOCUS ON FOOD

At left—Meatballs for any occasion. Clockwise from upper left: Saucy Meatballs (page 19), Batter-dipped Fondue Meatballs (page 28), Harvest-time Meatballs (page 20), Sweet-Sour Kabobs (this page).

SWEET-SOUR KABOBS

1½ pounds ground beef
 1 tablespoon soy sauce
 1 can (14½ ounces) sliced pineapple,
   drained (reserve syrup)
 2 tablespoons brown sugar
 2 tablespoons vinegar
 2 tablespoons soy sauce
 2 teaspoons cornstarch
 4 green onions, cut into 2-inch pieces
 1 small green pepper, cut into 1-inch
   pieces
12 cherry tomatoes

Mix meat and 1 tablespoon soy sauce. Shape mixture by tablespoonfuls into 36 balls. Place in glass bowl or plastic bag.

Mix reserved pineapple syrup, the brown sugar, vinegar and 2 tablespoons soy sauce until sugar is dissolved. Pour over meatballs. Cover and refrigerate at least 3 hours.

Drain marinade from meatballs into small saucepan; stir in cornstarch. Cook, stirring constantly, until mixture thickens and boils. Boil and stir 1 minute. Remove sauce from heat and set aside.

Cut pineapple slices into quarters. On each of six 12-inch metal skewers, alternate 6 meatballs with pineapple pieces and vegetables. Brush kabobs with part of the sauce.

Set oven control at broil and/or 550°. Broil kabobs 4 inches from heat to desired doneness, 15 to 20 minutes. Brush occasionally with sauce and gently push with fork to turn. (Pictured on page 26.)

6 servings.

BATTER-DIPPED FONDUE MEATBALLS

1½ pounds lean ground beef (chuck)
 1 egg
¼ cup dry bread crumbs
 2 tablespoons beer or apple juice
 1 teaspoon garlic salt
   Frothy Batter (below)
 2 cups salad oil
½ cup butter* (do not use margarine)
   Mustard Sauce (right) and Horseradish
   Sauce (right)

Mix meat, egg, bread crumbs, beer and garlic salt. Shape mixture by teaspoonfuls into ¾-inch balls. Prepare Frothy Batter.

Heat oil and butter in metal fondue pot to 375°. Spear meatballs with fondue forks, dip into batter and cook in hot oil to desired doneness, about 2 minutes. Serve with both sauces. (Pictured on page 26.)

About 7 dozen appetizer meatballs.

NOTE: These meatballs can also be cooked without the batter.

* You can omit the butter and increase salad oil to 2½ cups.

FROTHY BATTER
 1 cup biscuit baking mix
½ cup beer or apple juice
 1 egg

Mix all ingredients with fork. (Batter will be slightly lumpy.)

MUSTARD SAUCE

½ cup mayonnaise or salad dressing
 2 tablespoons prepared mustard
 1 tablespoon finely chopped onion

Mix all ingredients; refrigerate until serving time.

About ½ cup.

HORSERADISH SAUCE

½ cup dairy sour cream
 1 tablespoon horseradish
⅛ teaspoon Worcestershire sauce

Mix all ingredients; refrigerate until serving time.

About ½ cup.

APPETIZER MEATBALLS

Prepare Basic Meatballs (page 18) except—shape mixture by teaspoonfuls into ¾-inch balls and decrease cooking time to about 15 minutes. Serve with wooden or plastic picks.

48 appetizer meatballs.

PARTY-PLEASER MEATBALLS

    Basic Meatballs (page 18)
½ **cup flaked coconut**
¼ **cup currant or grape jelly**
¼ **cup chopped chutney or chutney sauce**
¼ **cup dry red wine or orange juice**
2 **teaspoons dry mustard**

Prepare Basic Meatballs except—add coconut before mixing ingredients. Shape mixture by teaspoonfuls into ¾-inch balls and bake in 400° oven 15 minutes. Drain off fat.

In large skillet, heat remaining ingredients to boiling. Add meatballs; cover and simmer, stirring occasionally, until sauce thickens and meatballs are glazed, about 20 minutes. Serve with wooden or plastic picks.

48 appetizer meatballs.

KEEP THE HEAT ON

When your party plans call for appetizer meatballs, make sure you keep them appetizing. And that means warm. Serve them from a chafing dish or from an electric skillet or saucepan. An attractive casserole on a warming tray will also do the trick. If your server's on the small side, it's a good idea to keep some of the meatballs on the range (over hot water) and refill the serving dish as the need arises.

COCKTAIL SURPRISE MEATBALLS

    Basic Meatballs (page 18)
1 **jar (5⅛ ounces) cocktail onions, drained***
¾ **cup catsup**
⅓ **cup grape or currant jelly**
⅓ **cup water**

Prepare Basic Meatballs except—shape mixture by teaspoonfuls around onions into 1-inch balls and bake in 400° oven 15 minutes. Drain off fat.

Combine catsup, jelly and water in large skillet. Add meatballs; heat to boiling, stirring occasionally. Reduce heat; cover and simmer 20 minutes, stirring occasionally. The onion centers are very hot, so be sure to let the meatballs cool slightly before serving with wooden or plastic picks.

48 appetizer meatballs.

* You can substitute drained pineapple tidbits or slices of small dill or sweet pickles for the cocktail onions.

Meat Loaves

Basic Meat Loaf

1½ pounds ground beef
3 slices bread, torn into small pieces*
1 egg
1 cup milk
1 small onion, chopped (about ¼ cup)
1 tablespoon Worcestershire sauce
1 teaspoon salt
½ teaspoon dry mustard
¼ teaspoon pepper
¼ teaspoon sage
⅛ teaspoon garlic powder
½ cup catsup, chili sauce or barbecue
　　sauce (optional)

Heat oven to 350°. Mix all ingredients except catsup. Spread mixture in ungreased loaf pan, 9×5×3 inches, or shape into loaf in ungreased baking pan. Spoon catsup onto loaf. Bake uncovered 1 to 1¼ hours. Drain off fat.

6 servings.

* You can substitute ½ cup dry bread crumbs, ½ cup wheat germ or ¾ cup quick-cooking oats for the bread pieces.

NOTE: If you have a microwave oven, see page 73 for specific instructions.

Have a freezer? See page 70 for Freezer Meat Loaf.

CHEESE-POTATO MEAT LOAF

Basic Meat Loaf (page 30)
¼ cup crumbled blue cheese
Instant mashed potato puffs
(enough for 4 servings)
Crumbled crisply fried bacon

Prepare Basic Meat Loaf except—mix in half the cheese and shape mixture into loaf in un-greased baking pan, 13×9×2 inches. Omit catsup and bake as directed. Drain off fat.

Prepare potato puffs as directed on package except—stir remaining cheese into potatoes. Spread potatoes on sides and top of meat loaf. Sprinkle with bacon and bake 10 minutes.

6 servings.

MEAT-AND-POTATO SQUARES

Basic Meat Loaf (page 30)
Instant mashed potato puffs
(enough for 4 servings)
½ cup shredded Cheddar cheese

Prepare Basic Meat Loaf except—spread mixture in ungreased baking pan, 8×8×2 or 9×9×2 inches. Omit catsup and decrease baking time to 40 to 50 minutes. Drain off fat.

Prepare potato puffs as directed on package. Spread hot potatoes evenly over meat in pan and sprinkle with cheese. Bake until cheese is melted, 2 to 4 minutes. (Pictured on page 23.)

6 servings.

Meat Loaf Leftovers

BARBECUE MEAT LOAF

For four ½-inch slices meat loaf, mix ½ cup bar-becue sauce and 2 tablespoons water in skillet. Place slices in skillet, turning to coat all sides with sauce. Heat to boiling. Cover and cook over low heat, brushing sauce on slices occasionally, until meat is hot, 10 to 15 minutes.

POTATO-TOPPED MEAT LOAF

For four ½-inch slices meat loaf, prepare instant mashed potato puffs as directed on package for 4 servings; set aside. Set oven control at broil and/or 550°. Broil slices with tops 3 to 4 inches from heat 5 minutes. Spread potatoes on slices and sprinkle with shredded Cheddar cheese. Broil until cheese is melted, about 2 minutes.

SOUPED-UP MEAT LOAF

For four ½-inch slices meat loaf, mix ½ to 1 can (10¾-ounce size) condensed cream of celery soup or any favorite condensed cream soup and ¼ to ½ cup milk in skillet. Heat to boiling, stirring frequently. Reduce heat; place slices in skillet, turning to coat all sides with sauce. Cover and simmer until meat is hot, 10 to 15 minutes.

ROAST MEAT LOAF

2 pounds ground beef
1 medium onion, chopped (about ½ cup)
1 egg
½ cup quick-cooking oats
½ cup milk
1 tablespoon snipped parsley
1½ teaspoons salt
½ teaspoon savory or thyme
¼ teaspoon pepper
½ cup catsup or chili sauce
2 tablespoons brown sugar

Heat oven to 350°. Mix all ingredients except catsup and brown sugar. Press mixture firmly in ungreased loaf pan, 8½×4½×2½ inches (see note). Loosen edges with spatula and un-mold loaf in ungreased baking pan, 13×9×2 inches. Mix catsup and sugar; spoon onto loaf. Bake uncovered 1 to 1¼ hours. (Pictured on the cover.)

8 servings.

NOTE: If you don't have a pan this size, shape mixture into loaf in center of shallow baking pan.

VARIATION

Roast Meat Loaf Ring: Press meat mixture firmly in ungreased 5- to 6-cup ring mold. Unmold in baking pan by rapping mold against bottom of pan. Brush with catsup mixture. Bake 50 minutes. If you like, fill the ring with hot potato salad or creamed peas.

ONION MEAT LOAF

2 pounds ground beef
1 envelope (about 1½ ounces) onion
  soup mix
⅔ cup milk
1 egg
3 tablespoons brown sugar
3 tablespoons catsup
1 tablespoon prepared mustard

Heat oven to 350°. Mix meat, onion soup mix, milk and egg. Press mixture firmly in ungreased loaf pan, 8½×4½×2½ inches (see note). Loosen edges with spatula and unmold loaf in ungreased baking pan, 13×9×2 inches.

Mix remaining ingredients; spoon onto loaf. Bake uncovered 1 hour. (Pictured on page 23.)

8 servings.

NOTE: If you don't have a pan this size, shape mixture into loaf in center of shallow baking pan.

DO AHEAD AND COAST LATER

Want to stamp out last-minute scurrying? Make your meat loaf mixture several hours in advance (or even the night before); spread it in the loaf pan, cover and refrigerate. When the dinner hour draws near, just pop the pan in the oven...and relax. Reminder: To compensate for the cold meat and the cold pan, you may have to add another 5 to 10 minutes to the baking time. (See page 70 for more information on freezing your meat loaf mixture.)

SAVORY STUFFED MEAT LOAF

1½ pounds ground beef
2 slices bacon, cut up
½ cup milk
1 egg
¼ cup dry bread crumbs
2 tablespoons snipped parsley
1 tablespoon Worcestershire sauce
1 teaspoon salt
½ teaspoon dry mustard
¼ teaspoon pepper
⅛ teaspoon garlic powder
   Meat Loaf Stuffing (below)

Heat oven to 350°. Mix all ingredients except stuffing. Spread ⅔ of the mixture in ungreased loaf pan, 9 × 5 × 3 inches, pressing mixture up sides of pan to within ¾ inch of top.

Spoon stuffing onto mixture in pan; then top with remaining meat mixture, covering stuffing completely. Bake uncovered 1 hour 10 minutes. Drain off fat. Let stuffed meat loaf stand 5 minutes before cutting into thick slices. (Pictured on page 23.)

6 servings.

MEAT LOAF STUFFING

¼ cup butter or margarine
1 small onion, chopped (about ¼ cup)
½ cup chopped celery (with leaves)
2 cups soft bread cubes
¼ teaspoon salt
¼ teaspoon sage
⅛ teaspoon thyme
   Dash pepper

Melt butter in large skillet. Add onion and celery; cook and stir until onion is tender. Remove from heat; stir in remaining ingredients.

ZUCCHINI-LAYERED MEAT LOAF

   Basic Meat Loaf (page 30)
½ cup shredded Swiss cheese
½ cup thinly sliced zucchini
2 tablespoons chopped pimiento

Prepare Basic Meat Loaf except—spread ⅓ of the mixture evenly in ungreased loaf pan, 9 × 5 × 3 inches. Sprinkle half each of the cheese, zucchini and pimiento in layers on mixture to within ½ inch of sides of pan; repeat. Top with remaining meat mixture, covering layers completely and spreading mixture to sides of pan. Omit catsup and bake uncovered 1¼ hours. Drain off fat. Let stuffed meat loaf stand 5 minutes before cutting into thick slices.

6 servings.

SPOONED-UP SKILLET MEAT LOAF

2 pounds ground beef
1 envelope (about 1½ ounces)
   onion soup mix
½ cup quick-cooking oats
½ cup water
½ cup dairy sour cream
2 eggs, beaten
¼ cup grated Parmesan cheese

Cook and stir meat in large skillet until brown. Drain off fat. Stir in soup mix, oats and water. Cover and simmer about 5 minutes, stirring occasionally. Stir in sour cream and eggs. Spread meat mixture evenly in skillet; sprinkle cheese over top. Cover and simmer until set, about 5 minutes. If desired, serve with catsup.

6 to 8 servings.

SURPRISE MEAT LOAF SQUARES

1½ pounds ground beef
 2 cups finely chopped pared eggplant
 1 medium onion, chopped (about ½ cup)
 1 egg
 ½ cup milk
 ¼ cup quick-cooking oats
1½ teaspoons salt
 ½ teaspoon basil leaves
 1 can (16 ounces) stewed tomatoes
 1 clove garlic, minced
 1 tablespoon cornstarch
 ¾ teaspoon salt

Heat oven to 350°. Mix meat, eggplant, onion, egg, milk, oats, 1½ teaspoons salt and the basil leaves. Spread mixture in ungreased baking pan, 8×8×2 or 9×9×2 inches. Bake uncovered 45 to 50 minutes. Drain off fat.

Mix tomatoes, garlic, cornstarch and ¾ teaspoon salt in small saucepan. Cook, stirring constantly, until mixture thickens and boils. Boil and stir 1 minute. Cut meat loaf into squares and top with tomato sauce.

6 servings.

SAUCY MINI-LOAVES

 1 pound ground beef (see note)
 ⅓ cup cracker crumbs
 1 can (10¾ ounces) condensed cream
   of mushroom soup
 ¼ cup milk
 1 egg
 1 small onion, chopped (about ¼ cup)
 ¾ teaspoon salt
 ⅛ teaspoon nutmeg
 ⅛ teaspoon pepper
 ½ cup chopped unpared cucumber
 3 tablespoons milk
 ⅓ cup chopped tomato
 ½ cup dairy sour cream

Heat oven to 350°. Mix meat, cracker crumbs, ½ cup of the soup, ¼ cup milk, the egg, onion and seasonings. Press mixture in 12 ungreased muffin cups. Bake 30 to 35 minutes.

In small saucepan, heat remaining soup, the cucumber and 3 tablespoons milk to boiling, stirring frequently. Reduce heat; stir in tomato and sour cream and heat just to boiling, stirring constantly. Serve sauce over mini-loaves.

4 to 6 servings.

NOTE: If ground beef is very fat, place muffin pan in a jelly roll pan to catch any juices that may cook over.

GIVE A LOAF A LIFT

The meat loaf is done—and it's a beauty! And you want to keep it that way. The simple trick is to use two wide spatulas to lift the loaf out of the pan. Simply sidle a spatula down each end of the pan and slip under the loaf. Then gently lift both ends—at the same time. Steady now.

MEAT LOAF TROPICALE

1½ pounds ground beef
 1 egg
 1 cup mashed ripe banana (about 2 large)
 ½ cup quick-cooking oats
 ½ cup chopped green pepper
 2 tablespoons chopped onion
 1 teaspoon salt
 1 teaspoon prepared mustard
 ¼ teaspoon nutmeg
 ⅛ teaspoon allspice
 2 slices bacon
 3 tablespoons orange marmalade

Heat oven to 350°. Mix all ingredients except bacon and marmalade. Spread mixture in ungreased loaf pan, 9×5×3 inches. Crisscross bacon slices on loaf, then spread marmalade on top. Bake uncovered 1 to 1¼ hours. Drain off fat.

6 servings.

NOTE: The banana adds a unique, almost mysterious flavor and a special moistness to this elegant meat loaf.

HEIDELBERG MEAT LOAF

1½ pounds ground beef
 3 slices rye bread, torn into small pieces
 1 cup beer or beef bouillon
 1 egg
 1 small onion, chopped (about ¼ cup)
 1 teaspoon salt
 1 teaspoon caraway seed (optional)
 ½ teaspoon celery seed
 ¼ teaspoon pepper

Heat oven to 350°. Mix all ingredients. Spread mixture in ungreased loaf pan, 9×5×3 inches. Bake uncovered 1 to 1¼ hours. Drain off fat.

6 servings.

BACON-WRAPPED LITTLE LOAVES

1½ pounds ground beef
 1 cup shredded Cheddar cheese (4 ounces)
 1 egg
 ¼ cup dry bread crumbs
 1 small onion, chopped (about ¼ cup)
 ¼ cup lemon juice
 ¼ chopped green pepper
 ½ cup water
 ½ teaspoon instant beef bouillon
 1 teaspoon salt
 6 slices thin-sliced bacon, cut into halves

Heat oven to 350°. Mix all ingredients except bacon. Shape mixture into 6 loaves. Crisscross 2 half-slices bacon on each loaf, tucking ends under loaf. Place loaves on rack in shallow baking pan; bake uncovered 50 minutes. (Pictured on page 23.)

6 servings.

Main Dishes

HAMBURGER STROGANOFF

1 pound ground beef
1 medium onion, chopped (about ½ cup)
1 clove garlic, minced
3 tablespoons flour
1 teaspoon instant beef bouillon
¾ teaspoon salt
¼ teaspoon pepper
1 can (4 ounces) mushroom stems and
   pieces, drained
1 cup water
1 cup dairy sour cream
2 cups hot cooked noodles or rice

Cook and stir meat, onion and garlic in large skillet until meat is brown. Drain off fat. Mix in flour, bouillon, salt, pepper and mushrooms. Stir in water and heat to boiling, stirring constantly. Reduce heat; cover and simmer 10 minutes. Stir in sour cream and heat. Serve over noodles; if you wish, garnish with parsley.

4 servings.

You can get a head start on this recipe with Beef-Mushroom Freezer Mix (see page 60).

SKILLET GOULASH

1 pound ground beef
1 medium onion, chopped (about ½ cup)
1 can (16 ounces) tomatoes
½ cup chopped celery
½ cup water
1½ teaspoons salt
¼ teaspoon pepper
⅛ teaspoon basil leaves
⅛ teaspoon marjoram leaves
3 ounces uncooked fine noodles
   (about 1½ cups)

Cook and stir meat and onion in large skillet until meat is brown. Drain off fat. Stir in tomatoes (with liquid) and remaining ingredients; break up tomatoes.

Heat to boiling. Reduce heat; cover and simmer, stirring occasionally, until noodles are tender, about 20 minutes. (A small amount of water can be added if necessary.)

5 servings (1 cup each).

You can get a head start on this recipe with Browned 'n Seasoned Freezer Mix (see page 63).

ALL-AMERICAN HOT DISH

1 pound ground beef
1 medium onion, chopped (about ½ cup)
1 can (8 ounces) whole kernel corn
1 can (8 ounces) tomato sauce
¼ cup halved pitted ripe olives
4 ounces uncooked noodles (about 2 cups)
2 cups water
1 teaspoon oregano leaves
½ teaspoon salt
¼ teaspoon pepper
1 cup shredded Cheddar cheese (4 ounces)

Cook and stir meat and onion in large skillet until meat is brown. Drain off fat. Stir in corn (with liquid) and remaining ingredients.

TO COOK IN SKILLET: Heat mixture to boiling. Reduce heat and simmer uncovered, stirring occasionally, until noodles are tender, about 20 minutes.

TO COOK IN OVEN: Pour mixture into ungreased 2-quart casserole. Cover and bake in 375° oven 30 minutes, stirring occasionally. Uncover and bake until mixture thickens, about 15 minutes.

6 servings (1 cup each).

You can get a head start on this recipe with Browned 'n Seasoned Freezer Mix (see page 63).

PASTA: HOW MUCH TO COOK?

Macaroni, spaghetti or noodles—take your pick. For 2 cups of cooked pasta, start with:
1 cup macaroni (3 to 3½ ounces)
3½ to 4 ounces spaghetti
2 to 2½ cups noodles (4 ounces)

CREAMY BEEF-NOODLE COMBO

1 pound ground beef
1 medium onion, chopped (about ½ cup)
1 can (4 ounces) mushroom stems and pieces
1 can (10¾ ounces) condensed cream of mushroom soup
2 stalks celery, sliced (about 1 cup)
½ cup chopped green pepper
¼ cup sliced pimiento
1 cup milk
1 tablespoon Worcestershire sauce
1 teaspoon salt
4 ounces uncooked noodles (about 2 cups)

Cook and stir meat and onion in large skillet until meat is brown. Drain off fat. Stir in mushrooms (with liquid) and remaining ingredients; heat to boiling. Reduce heat; cover and simmer, stirring occasionally, until noodles are tender, about 25 minutes. A small amount of water can be added if necessary. (Pictured on page 54.)

5 servings (1 cup each).

You can get a head start on this recipe with Browned 'n Seasoned Freezer Mix (see page 63).

NOTE: If you have a microwave oven, be sure to see page 74 for specific instructions.

DOUBLE CHEESE HAMBURGER CASSEROLE

4 ounces uncooked medium noodles (about 2 cups)
1 pound ground beef
⅓ cup chopped onion
¼ cup chopped celery
1 can (8 ounces) tomato sauce
1 teaspoon salt
1 package (3 ounces) cream cheese, softened
½ cup creamed cottage cheese
¼ cup dairy sour cream
1 medium tomato (optional)

Cook noodles as directed on package; drain. While noodles are cooking, cook and stir meat, onion and celery in large skillet until meat is brown. Drain off fat. Stir in noodles, tomato sauce, salt, cream cheese, cottage cheese and sour cream.

TO COOK IN SKILLET: Heat mixture to boiling. Reduce heat and simmer uncovered 5 minutes, stirring frequently. Remove from heat. Cut tomato into thin slices and arrange on meat mixture. Cover until tomato slices are warm, about 5 minutes.

TO COOK IN OVEN: Turn mixture into ungreased 1½-quart casserole. Cut tomato into thin slices and arrange on meat mixture. Cover and bake in 350° oven until hot, about 30 minutes.

5 servings (1 cup each).

LASAGNE

MEAT SAUCE

1 pound ground beef
2 cloves garlic, minced
3 cans (8 ounces each) tomato sauce*
½ teaspoon salt
¼ teaspoon pepper
½ teaspoon oregano leaves

NOODLES AND CHEESE

1 package (8 ounces) lasagne noodles
1 carton (12 ounces) creamed cottage cheese (1½ cups)
2 cups shredded mozzarella or Swiss cheese (8 ounces)
⅓ cup grated Parmesan cheese

Cook and stir meat and garlic in large skillet until meat is brown. Drain off fat. Stir in tomato sauce, salt, pepper and oregano leaves. Cover and simmer 20 minutes.

While Meat Sauce is simmering, cook noodles as directed on package; drain.

Heat oven to 350°. In ungreased baking pan, 13×9×2 inches, or baking dish, 11¾×7½×1¾ inches, layer half each of the noodles, meat sauce, cottage cheese and mozzarella cheese; repeat. Sprinkle Parmesan cheese over top. Bake uncovered until hot and bubbly, about 40 minutes.

6 servings.

*You can substitute 1 can (16 ounces) tomatoes and 1 can (6 ounces) tomato paste for the tomato sauce.

Like to plan ahead? See page 70 for Freezer Lasagne. Or get a head start with Beef-Tomato Freezer Mix (see page 66).

ITALIAN SPAGHETTI

2 pounds ground beef
1 medium onion, chopped (about ½ cup)
2 cans (15 ounces each) tomato sauce
2 cans (12 ounces each) tomato paste
1 can (7½ ounces) pitted ripe olives,
   drained and sliced (½ cup)
2 envelopes (about 1½ ounces each) Italian-
   style spaghetti sauce mix with
   mushrooms
1 cup chopped green pepper
3 cups water
1 tablespoon sugar
1 teaspoon oregano leaves
2 cloves garlic, minced
1 bay leaf
14 to 16 ounces uncooked long spaghetti
   Grated Parmesan cheese

Cook and stir meat and onion in large skillet or Dutch oven until meat is brown. Drain off fat. Stir in remaining ingredients except spaghetti and cheese; heat to boiling. Reduce heat; cover and simmer 1½ hours, stirring occasionally. Remove bay leaf. Cook spaghetti as directed on package; drain. Serve sauce over spaghetti and sprinkle with Parmesan cheese.

8 servings.

ONE-SKILLET SPAGHETTI

1 pound ground beef
2 medium onions, chopped (about 1 cup)
1 can (28 ounces) tomatoes
¾ cup chopped green pepper
½ cup water
1 can (4 ounces) mushroom stems
   and pieces, drained
2 teaspoons salt
1 teaspoon sugar
1 teaspoon chili powder
1 package (7 ounces) thin spaghetti,
   broken into pieces
1 cup shredded Cheddar cheese
   (4 ounces)

Cook and stir meat and onions in large skillet or Dutch oven until meat is brown. Drain off fat. Stir in tomatoes (with liquid) and remaining ingredients except Cheddar cheese; break up tomatoes.

TO COOK IN SKILLET: Heat mixture to boiling. Reduce heat; cover and simmer, stirring occasionally, until spaghetti is tender, about 30 minutes. (A small amount of water can be added if necessary.) Sprinkle with cheese. Cover and heat until cheese is melted.

TO COOK IN OVEN: Pour mixture into ungreased 2- or 2½-quart casserole. Cover and bake in 375° oven, stirring occasionally, until spaghetti is tender, about 45 minutes. Uncover; sprinkle with shredded Cheddar cheese and bake about 5 minutes.

7 servings (1 cup each).

You can get a head start on this recipe with Beef-Tomato Freezer Mix (see page 66).

MANICOTTI

MEAT FILLING
- 1 pound ground beef
- ¼ cup chopped onion (about 1 small)
- 3 slices bread, torn into small pieces
- 1½ cups shredded mozzarella cheese
- 1 egg
- ½ cup milk
- 1 tablespoon snipped parsley
- 1 teaspoon salt
- ¼ teaspoon pepper

PASTA
1 package (8 ounces) manicotti shells

TOMATO SAUCE
- 1 can (4 ounces) mushroom stems and pieces
- 1 can (15 ounces) tomato sauce
- 1 can (12 ounces) tomato paste
- ¼ cup chopped onion (about 1 small)
- 1 clove garlic, minced
- 4 cups water
- 1 tablespoon Italian seasoning
- ½ teaspoon sugar
- ½ teaspoon salt
- ⅛ teaspoon pepper
- ⅓ cup grated Parmesan cheese

Cook and stir meat and ¼ cup onion in large skillet until meat is brown. Drain off fat. Remove from heat; stir in remaining ingredients for Meat Filling.

Fill uncooked manicotti shells, packing the filling into both ends. Place shells in ungreased baking pan, 13 × 9 × 2 inches.

Heat oven to 375°. Heat mushrooms (with liquid) and remaining ingredients for Tomato Sauce except cheese to boiling, stirring occasionally. Reduce heat and simmer uncovered 5 minutes. Pour sauce over shells. Cover with aluminum foil and bake until shells are tender, 1½ to 1¾ hours. Sprinkle with cheese. Cool 5 to 10 minutes before serving.

6 to 8 servings.

Have a freezer? See page 71 for Freezer Manicotti.

MEXICAN FIESTA CASSEROLE
- 1 pound ground beef
- Salt and pepper
- 1 cup shredded Cheddar cheese (4 ounces)
- 1 cup dairy sour cream
- ⅔ cup mayonnaise or salad dressing
- 2 tablespoons finely chopped onion
- 2 cups biscuit baking mix
- ½ cup water
- 2 to 3 medium tomatoes, thinly sliced
- ¾ cup chopped green pepper
- Paprika (optional)

Heat oven to 375°. Cook and stir meat in skillet until brown. Drain off fat. Season meat with salt and pepper; set aside. Mix cheese, sour cream, mayonnaise and onion; set aside.

Stir baking mix and water until a soft dough forms. With floured fingers, pat dough in greased baking pan, 13 × 9 × 2 inches, pressing dough ½ inch up sides of pan. Layer meat, tomato slices and green pepper on dough. Spoon sour cream mixture over top and sprinkle with paprika. Bake uncovered until edges of dough are light brown, 25 to 30 minutes. Cool 5 minutes, then cut into squares.

5 or 6 servings.

ENCHILADAS

MEAT FILLING

1 pound ground beef
1 medium onion, chopped (about ½ cup)
½ cup dairy sour cream
1 cup shredded Cheddar cheese (4 ounces)
2 tablespoons snipped parsley
1 teaspoon salt
¼ teaspoon pepper

TORTILLA BASE

  Salad oil
8 tortillas

HOT TOMATO SAUCE

 1 can (15 ounces) tomato sauce
 ⅓ cup chopped green pepper
 1 clove garlic, minced
1½ to 2 teaspoons chili powder
 ½ teaspoon oregano leaves
 ¼ teaspoon ground cumin
 ⅔ cup water

Cook and stir meat in large skillet until brown. Drain off fat. Stir in remaining ingredients for Meat Filling. Remove from heat; cover and set aside.

Heat ¼ inch salad oil in skillet over medium heat. Dip each tortilla quickly into oil, turning once with tongs, just until limp; drain on paper towel.

In small saucepan, heat all ingredients for Hot Tomato Sauce except water to boiling, stirring occasionally. Reduce heat and simmer uncovered 5 minutes. Pour sauce into 8- or 9-inch shallow dish.

Heat oven to 350°. Dip each tortilla into sauce to coat both sides; place about ¼ cup Meat Filling on center and roll tortilla around filling. Arrange in ungreased baking dish, 11¾ × 7½ × 1¾ inches. Pour remaining sauce and the water over tortillas. Bake uncovered until bubbly, about 20 minutes. If you wish, garnish with slices of ripe olives, avocado, hard-cooked egg or shredded lettuce. (Pictured on page 51.)

4 or 5 servings.

Have a freezer? See page 71 for Freezer Enchiladas.

A BIT ABOUT TORTILLAS

The Mexicans know all about the care and handling of the tortilla, their traditional flat, unleavened bread. So take a tip from south of the border. When it comes to making Enchiladas, it's best to dip the tortillas in oil first—it makes them soft and easy to roll. Then drain off the excess oil so that the zesty sauce will cling to the surface. And this holds true whether you have chosen either corn or flour tortillas—canned, frozen or refrigerated.

The tortilla is also the basis for the taco shell, which you can purchase already crisply fried and folded into a half-moon shape—ready for its many fillings.

COMPANY BEEF ORIENTAL

1½ pounds ground beef
 1 medium onion, sliced
 1 clove garlic, minced
 ¼ cup soy sauce
 2 tablespoons cornstarch
 1 tablespoon molasses
 1 teaspoon instant beef bouillon
 ¾ cup water
 1 package (6 ounces) frozen Chinese
   pea pods
 1 can (5 ounces) water chestnuts, drained
   and sliced
 1 can (5 ounces) bamboo shoots, drained
 1 can (11 ounces) mandarin orange
   segments, drained (reserve syrup)

Cook and stir meat, onion and garlic in large skillet until meat is brown. Drain off fat. Mix soy sauce, cornstarch and molasses; stir into meat mixture. Stir in bouillon, water, pea pods, water chestnuts, bamboo shoots and reserved mandarin orange syrup; heat to boiling.

Reduce heat; cover and simmer 10 minutes, stirring occasionally. Stir in orange segments; cover and heat about 2 minutes.

Nice served with hot cooked rice and additional soy sauce. (Pictured on the cover.)

6 servings (1 cup each).

SAFARI SUPPER

1½ pounds ground beef
 1 medium onion, sliced
 1 cup uncooked regular rice
2½ cups water
 2 teaspoons instant chicken bouillon
 1 teaspoon curry powder
 ½ teaspoon salt
 ¼ teaspoon ginger
 ¼ teaspoon cinnamon
 3 tablespoons chunky peanut butter
 1 tablespoon honey
 ½ cup raisins

Cook and stir meat and onion in large skillet until onion is tender. Drain off fat. Stir in remaining ingredients.

TO COOK IN SKILLET: Heat mixture to boiling. Reduce heat; cover and simmer, stirring occasionally, until rice is tender, about 35 minutes. (A small amount of water can be added if necessary.)

TO COOK IN OVEN: Turn mixture into ungreased 2-quart casserole. Cover and bake in 350° oven, stirring occasionally, until rice is tender, 50 to 60 minutes. (A small amount of water can be added if necessary.)

8 servings (1 cup each).

SPANISH RICE WITH BEEF

- 1 pound ground beef
- 1 medium onion, chopped (about ½ cup)
- 1 cup uncooked regular rice
- ⅔ cup chopped green pepper
- 1 can (16 ounces) stewed tomatoes
- 5 slices bacon, crisply fried and crumbled
- 2 cups water
- 1 teaspoon chili powder
- ½ teaspoon oregano leaves
- 1¼ teaspoons salt
- ⅛ teaspoon pepper

Cook and stir meat and onion in large skillet until meat is brown. Drain off fat. Stir in remaining ingredients.

TO COOK IN SKILLET: Heat mixture to boiling. Reduce heat; cover and simmer, stirring occasionally, until rice is tender, about 30 minutes. (A small amount of water can be added if necessary.)

TO COOK IN OVEN: Pour mixture into ungreased 2-quart casserole. Cover and bake in 375° oven, stirring occasionally, until rice is tender, about 45 minutes.

6 servings (1 cup each).

You can get a head start on this recipe with Beef-Tomato Freezer Mix (see page 65).

RUNDOWN ON RICE

Heed the following chart for the rice of your choice. For 2 cups cooked rice, start with:

⅔ cup regular white rice
½ cup processed rice
1 cup precooked (instant) rice
½ cup brown rice

HEARTY BEEF SUPPER

- 2 pounds ground beef
- 1 large onion, chopped (about 1 cup)
- 1 cup uncooked cracked wheat (see note)
- 2 cups chopped tomato (about 2 medium)
- 2 cups water
- 3 tablespoons snipped parsley
- 2 teaspoons instant beef bouillon
- 1½ teaspoons salt
- ½ teaspoon oregano leaves
- ¼ teaspoon instant minced garlic
- ¼ teaspoon pepper
- ½ cup grated Parmesan cheese

Cook and stir meat and onion in large skillet until meat is brown. Drain off fat. Stir in remaining ingredients except cheese; heat to boiling. Reduce heat; cover and simmer, stirring occasionally, until wheat is tender, about 30 minutes. (A small amount of water can be added if necessary.) Stir in cheese. Garnish with additional snipped parsley and Parmesan cheese.

7 servings (1 cup each).

NOTE: The nutlike texture of cracked wheat reminds one of brown rice; in fact, it is cooked and used in the same way too.

SOUTH SEAS COMBO

  2 pounds ground beef
  1 medium onion, chopped (about ½ cup)
  1 cup sliced celery
2½ cups coarsely chopped pared apple
  2 to 3 teaspoons curry powder
  2 tablespoons flour
  2 teaspoons instant beef bouillon
  1 cup water
  1 can (4 ounces) mushroom stems and
     pieces, drained
  2 tablespoons sherry (optional)
  2 bananas, peeled and sliced*
  4 cups hot cooked rice

Cook and stir meat and onion in large skillet until onion is tender. Drain off fat. Stir in celery, apple and curry powder; cook uncovered 5 minutes, stirring occasionally. Stir in remaining ingredients except bananas and rice; heat to boiling. Reduce heat and simmer uncovered about 30 minutes, stirring occasionally.

Stir in bananas; cover and cook over low heat 5 minutes. Serve over rice. If you wish, garnish with crumbled crisply fried bacon or chopped peanuts.

8 servings.

*You can substitute 1 can (13½ ounces) pineapple chunks, drained, for the sliced bananas.

CURRY DELIGHT

  2 pounds ground beef
  1 large onion, chopped (about 1 cup)
  1 can (16 ounces) tomatoes
  1 large apple, chopped (about 1¼ cups)
  1 to 1½ tablespoons curry powder
  2 tablespoons coconut (optional)
  2 tablespoons raisins
  1 tablespoon chopped chutney
  2 teaspoons instant beef bouillon
1½ teaspoons salt
  1 cup uncooked regular rice
2½ cups water
     Chopped peanuts

Cook and stir meat and onion in Dutch oven until meat is brown. Drain off fat. Stir in tomatoes (with liquid) and remaining ingredients except peanuts; break up tomatoes.

TO COOK IN DUTCH OVEN: Heat mixture to boiling. Reduce heat; cover and simmer, stirring occasionally, until rice is tender, 30 to 45 minutes. (A small amount of water can be added if necessary.) Garnish with peanuts.

TO COOK IN OVEN: Turn mixture into ungreased 3-quart casserole. Cover and bake in 350° oven, stirring occasionally, until rice is tender, 45 to 55 minutes. Garnish with peanuts.

7 servings (1 cup each).

APPLE-FILLED SQUASH HALVES

2 acorn squash
1 pound ground beef*
1½ teaspoons salt
½ teaspoon cinnamon
2 tart apples, pared and coarsely chopped
  (about 2 cups)
¼ cup raisins
  Salt
4 tablespoons brown sugar
2 tablespoons butter or margarine,
  melted

Heat oven to 400°. Cut each squash in half; remove seeds and fibers. Place halves cut sides down in ungreased baking pan. Add water to a depth of ¼ inch. Bake uncovered until squash is tender, 30 to 40 minutes.

While squash is baking, cook and stir meat in large skillet until brown. Drain off fat. Remove skillet from heat; stir in 1½ teaspoons salt, the cinnamon, apples and raisins.

Turn squash halves cut sides up; drain any remaining liquid from baking pan. Scoop out pulp from shells, leaving a ¼-inch-thick wall in each. Season shells with salt.

Mash pulp; mix into meat mixture and pile into shells. Sprinkle 1 tablespoon brown sugar over each and drizzle with butter. Bake uncovered until apple is tender, 20 to 30 minutes. (Pictured on page 51.)

4 servings.

*You can substitute a combination of ½ pound ground beef and ½ pound bulk pork sausage for the 1 pound ground beef.

STUFFED GREEN PEPPERS

PEPPER SHELLS
3 large green peppers
5 cups boiling salted water

MEAT FILLING
1 pound ground beef
1 small onion, chopped (about ¼ cup)
½ cup chopped celery
1 can (8 ounces) tomato sauce
1 teaspoon salt
¼ teaspoon garlic salt
1 teaspoon Worcestershire sauce
½ cup uncooked instant rice
½ cup water

Heat oven to 350°. Cut each pepper lengthwise in half. Wash insides and outsides; remove seeds and membranes. Cook peppers in boiling salted water 5 minutes. Drain and set aside.

Cook and stir meat, onion and celery in large skillet until meat is brown. Drain off fat. Stir in half the tomato sauce and the remaining ingredients; heat to boiling. Reduce heat; cover and simmer 5 minutes.

Place peppers cut sides up in ungreased baking pan, 9×9×2 or 8×8×2 inches. Spoon Meat Filling into peppers. Cover with aluminum foil and bake 25 minutes. Uncover; top with remaining tomato sauce and bake 5 minutes.

4 or 5 servings.

Like to plan ahead? See page 71 for Freezer Stuffed Green Peppers.

STUFFED CABBAGE ROLLS

    9 cups water
   12 cabbage leaves (see note)
    1 pound lean ground beef (chuck)
   ½ cup uncooked instant rice
    1 medium onion, chopped (about ½ cup)
    1 can (4 ounces) mushroom stems and
      pieces
    1 teaspoon salt
   ⅛ teaspoon pepper
   ⅛ teaspoon garlic salt
    1 can (15 ounces) tomato sauce
    1 teaspoon sugar
   ½ teaspoon lemon juice
    1 tablespoon cornstarch
    1 tablespoon water

In Dutch oven or large saucepan, heat 9 cups water to boiling. Place cabbage leaves in boiling water; remove from heat. Cover and let stand until leaves are softened, about 10 minutes.

Mix meat, rice, onion, mushrooms (with liquid), seasonings and ½ cup of the tomato sauce. Remove cabbage leaves from water; drain. Place about ⅓ cup meat mixture at stem end of each leaf. Roll leaf around meat mixture, tucking in sides.

TO COOK IN SKILLET: Place rolls seam sides down in large skillet. Mix remaining tomato sauce, the sugar and lemon juice; pour over rolls and heat to boiling. Reduce heat; cover and simmer until meat is cooked, about 45 minutes. Remove cabbage rolls to warm platter. Mix cornstarch and 1 tablespoon water; stir into liquid in skillet. Cook, stirring constantly, until mixture thickens and boils. Boil and stir 1 minute. Serve sauce over cabbage rolls, and if you wish, garnish with lemon slices and parsley.

TO COOK IN OVEN: Place rolls seam sides down in ungreased baking pan, 9×9×2 inches. Mix remaining tomato sauce, the sugar and lemon juice; pour over rolls. Cover with aluminum foil and bake in 350° oven until meat is cooked, about 45 minutes. Mix cornstarch and 1 tablespoon water in small saucepan. Stir in liquid from cabbage rolls. Cook, stirring constantly, until mixture thickens and boils. Boil and stir 1 minute. Serve sauce over cabbage rolls, and if you wish, garnish with lemon slices and parsley.

4 to 6 servings.

NOTE: To separate leaves from cabbage head easily, cover the head with cold water and let stand about 10 minutes; then remove leaves.

SPICED BEAN BAKE

    1 pound ground beef
    1 small onion, chopped (about ¼ cup)
    1 apple, chopped
    1 teaspoon curry powder
   ½ teaspoon dry mustard
    1 can (28 ounces) baked beans in molasses
      sauce with pork
    1 apple, sliced

Heat oven to 350°. Cook and stir meat and onion in large skillet until meat is brown. Drain off fat. Stir in chopped apple, the curry powder, mustard and beans; turn into ungreased 1½-quart casserole. Arrange apple slices on top. Cover and bake until hot, 25 to 35 minutes.

5 servings (1 cup each).

SOUPER BAKED SANDWICH

1½ pounds ground beef
 1 small onion, chopped (about ¼ cup)
½ cup chopped celery
½ teaspoon salt
 4 cups herb-seasoned stuffing cubes
1½ cups milk
 2 eggs
 1 can (10¾ ounces) condensed cream of
   mushroom soup
 1 teaspoon dry mustard
 1 cup shredded Cheddar cheese (4 ounces)

Heat oven to 350°. Cook and stir meat, onion and celery in large skillet until meat is brown. Drain off fat. Stir in salt.

Arrange stuffing cubes in greased baking pan, 9×9×2 or 11¾×7½×1¾ inches; top with meat mixture. Beat milk, eggs, soup and mustard; pour over meat and sprinkle with cheese. Bake uncovered until knife inserted in center comes out clean, 30 to 40 minutes. Cool 5 minutes, then cut into squares.

About 6 servings.

MEXICALI SPOON BREAD CASSEROLE

MEAT MIXTURE
1½ pounds ground beef
 1 large onion, chopped (about 1 cup)
¼ cup chopped green pepper (optional)
 1 clove garlic, minced
 1 can (15 ounces) tomato sauce
 1 can (12 ounces) vacuum-pack whole
   kernel corn
1½ teaspoons salt
 2 to 3 teaspoons chili powder
⅛ teaspoon pepper
½ cup sliced ripe olives

CORNMEAL TOPPING
1½ cups milk
½ cup yellow cornmeal
½ teaspoon salt
¾ cup shredded Cheddar cheese
 2 eggs, beaten

Heat oven to 375°. Cook and stir meat, onion, green pepper and garlic in large skillet until onion is tender. Drain off fat. Stir in tomato sauce, corn (with liquid), 1½ teaspoons salt, the chili powder, pepper and olives; heat to boiling. Reduce heat and simmer uncovered while preparing Cornmeal Topping.

Mix milk, cornmeal and ½ teaspoon salt in saucepan. Cook and stir over medium heat just until mixture boils. Remove from heat; stir in cheese and eggs.

Turn hot Meat Mixture into ungreased 2½- to 3-quart casserole. Immediately pour topping onto Meat Mixture. Bake uncovered until knife inserted in topping comes out clean, about 40 minutes.

6 to 8 servings.

SAUCY BEAN 'N BEEF PIE

1 pound ground beef
1 can (3½ ounces) French fried onions
¼ cup dry bread crumbs
1 can (10¾ ounces) condensed cream of
    mushroom soup
1 egg
¼ teaspoon thyme leaves
¼ teaspoon salt
    Dash pepper
1 can (16 ounces) French-style green beans,
    drained

Heat oven to 350°. Mix meat, half the onions, the bread crumbs, ¼ cup of the soup, the egg, thyme leaves, salt and pepper. Press mixture evenly against bottom and side of ungreased 9-inch pie pan.

Turn beans into meat-lined pan; spread remaining soup over beans. Bake uncovered 35 minutes. Arrange remaining onions on top; bake 10 minutes. Cool 5 minutes, then cut into wedges.

4 or 5 servings.

CHEESEBURGER PIE

CRUST
1 cup biscuit baking mix
¼ cup milk or light cream

MEAT FILLING
1 pound ground beef
1 medium onion, chopped (about ½ cup)
½ teaspoon salt
¼ teaspoon pepper
2 tablespoons biscuit baking mix
1 tablespoon Worcestershire sauce

TOPPING
2 medium tomatoes, sliced
2 eggs
1 cup shredded Cheddar cheese (4 ounces)

Heat oven to 375°. Mix 1 cup baking mix and the milk until a soft dough forms. Gently smooth dough into a ball on floured cloth-covered surface; knead 5 times. Roll dough 2 inches larger than inverted 9-inch pie pan. Ease into pan and flute edge of dough.

Cook and stir meat and onion in large skillet until meat is brown. Drain off fat. Stir in salt, pepper, 2 tablespoons baking mix and the Worcestershire sauce. Turn Meat Filling into pastry-lined pan.

Arrange tomato slices on filling. Beat eggs slightly; stir in cheese. Spoon onto tomatoes, spreading to cover completely. Bake about 30 minutes. Cut into wedges. Serve with chili sauce if you like.

6 servings.

You can get a head start on this recipe with Browned 'n Seasoned Freezer Mix (see page 63).

PEPPY PIZZA PIE

1 pound ground beef
2 ounces pepperoni, chopped (about ⅓ cup)
⅓ cup dry bread crumbs
1 egg
½ teaspoon oregano leaves
¼ teaspoon salt
1 can (8 ounces) tomato sauce
1 can (8 ounces) mushroom stems and pieces, drained*
¼ cup sliced pitted ripe olives
1 cup shredded mozzarella cheese (4 ounces)

Heat oven to 400°. Mix meats, bread crumbs, egg, oregano leaves, salt and half the tomato sauce. Press mixture evenly against bottom and side of ungreased 10-inch pie pan (see note).

Sprinkle mushrooms and olives in meat-lined pan; pour remaining tomato sauce over vegetables. Bake uncovered 25 minutes. (The pepperoni gives a red-flecked appearance to the meat.) Sprinkle pie with cheese; bake 5 minutes. Cool 5 minutes, then cut into 6 wedges.

6 servings.

* You can substitute 1 can (8 ounces) cut green beans, drained, or 1 can (8 ounces) whole kernel corn, drained, for the mushrooms.

NOTE: If you have to use a 9-inch pie pan, place it in a shallow baking pan to catch any juices that may cook over.

POTLUCK SURPRISE

1½ cups uncooked elbow macaroni
1½ pounds ground beef
1 medium onion, chopped (about ½ cup)
1½ teaspoons salt
1 teaspoon Italian seasoning
¼ teaspoon pepper
1 small eggplant, pared and cut into ½-inch cubes (about 4 cups)
1 cup dairy sour cream
¼ cup chopped pimiento*
2 cups shredded Cheddar cheese (8 ounces)

Heat oven to 350°. Cook macaroni as directed on package; drain. While macaroni is cooking, cook and stir meat and onion in Dutch oven until meat is brown. Drain off fat. Stir in salt, Italian seasoning, pepper, macaroni, eggplant, sour cream, pimiento and 1 cup of the cheese.

Turn into ungreased 3-quart casserole. Sprinkle with remaining cheese. Bake uncovered until eggplant is tender, 45 to 50 minutes.

6 to 8 servings.

*You can substitute ½ cup sliced pimiento-stuffed olives for the chopped pimiento.

BEEF MOUSSAKA

1½ pounds ground beef
 1 medium onion, chopped (about ½ cup)
 2 tablespoons snipped parsley
 1 teaspoon salt
 ¼ teaspoon pepper
 ⅛ teaspoon nutmeg
 1 can (8 ounces) tomato sauce
 ¼ cup dry red wine or tomato juice
 1 medium eggplant
 6 eggs
 ¾ cup milk
 ½ teaspoon salt
 ⅓ cup grated Parmesan cheese

Heat oven to 375°. Cook and stir meat and onion in large skillet until meat is brown. Drain off fat. Stir in parsley, 1 teaspoon salt, the pepper, nutmeg, tomato sauce and wine; heat to boiling. Reduce heat and simmer uncovered 5 minutes.

Pare eggplant and cut into ½-inch slices. Arrange half the eggplant slices in ungreased baking dish, 11¾ × 7½ × 1¾ inches; top with half the meat mixture. Repeat with remaining eggplant slices and meat mixture. Cover with aluminum foil and bake until eggplant is tender, about 40 minutes.

Beat eggs, milk and ½ teaspoon salt; pour over hot casserole and sprinkle with cheese. Bake uncovered until custard is set, 10 to 15 minutes. Cool 10 minutes, then cut into squares. (Pictured on page 51.)

8 servings.

HUNGRY BOY'S CASSEROLE

1 pound ground beef
 2 stalks celery, sliced (about 1 cup)
 1 medium onion, chopped (about ½ cup)
 1 clove garlic, minced
 1 can (16 ounces) garbanzo or lima beans
 1 can (16 ounces) pork and beans
 ½ cup chopped green pepper
 1 teaspoon salt
 1 can (6 ounces) tomato paste

Cook and stir meat, celery, onion and garlic in large skillet until meat is brown. Drain off fat. Stir in garbanzo beans (with liquid) and remaining ingredients.

TO COOK IN SKILLET: Heat mixture to boiling. Reduce heat; cover and simmer 10 minutes, stirring occasionally.

TO COOK IN OVEN: Pour mixture into ungreased 2-quart casserole. Cover and bake in 375° oven until hot and bubbly, about 45 minutes.

6 servings (1 cup each).

FOCUS ON FOOD

At right—Hamburger dishes for family or company. Clockwise from top: Apple-filled Squash Halves (page 45), Enchiladas (page 41), Beef Moussaka (this page).

On page 52—With Browned 'n Seasoned Freezer Mix: Freezer Mix Pizzawiches (page 63), Freezer Mix Cheeseburger Pie (page 63).

On page 53—With Beef-Tomato Freezer Mix: Freezer Mix Lentil Stew (page 67), Freezer Mix One-dish Spaghetti (page 66).

CHILI-RONI

1 pound ground beef
2 medium onions, chopped (about
   1 cup)
1 can (15½ ounces) kidney beans
1 can (28 ounces) tomatoes
1 can (8 ounces) tomato sauce
1 cup chopped green pepper (optional)
1 cup uncooked elbow macaroni
2 to 4 teaspoons chili powder
1 teaspoon salt
⅛ teaspoon cayenne red pepper
⅛ teaspoon paprika

Cook and stir meat and onions in large skillet or Dutch oven until meat is brown. Drain off fat. Stir in kidney beans (with liquid), tomatoes (with liquid) and remaining ingredients; break up tomatoes.

Heat to boiling. Reduce heat; cover and simmer, stirring occasionally, until macaroni is tender, 20 to 30 minutes. If you prefer a thinner consistency, add water or wine.

6 servings (1⅓ cups each).

VARIATION

Chili con Carne: Omit elbow macaroni and simmer uncovered until of desired consistency, about 30 minutes.

FOCUS ON FOOD

At left—Hearty and handsome casserole fare. Clockwise from top: Minnesota Minestrone (page 57), Muffin-topped Chili (this page), Creamy Beef-Noodle Combo (page 37).

MUFFIN-TOPPED CHILI

  Chili con Carne (left)
1 cup biscuit baking mix
2 tablespoons cornmeal
1 egg
⅓ cup milk
1 tablespoon cornmeal

Prepare Chili con Carne except—decrease simmering time to 15 minutes.

Heat oven to 425°. Mix baking mix, 2 tablespoons cornmeal, the egg and milk; beat vigorously ½ minute. Pour hot Chili con Carne into ungreased 3-quart casserole. Drop batter by spoonfuls around edge of casserole; sprinkle batter with 1 tablespoon cornmeal. Bake uncovered 25 minutes. (Pictured on page 54.)

6 to 8 servings.

VEGETABLE BEEF NOODLE DINNER

1 package (10 ounces) frozen green peas
1 can (10½ ounces) condensed beef broth
   (bouillon)
1 package (7 ounces) mix for beef noodle
   dinner
2 tablespoons chopped pimiento

Rinse frozen peas with small amount of running cold water to separate and remove ice crystals; set aside. Add enough water to beef broth to measure 3¼ cups.

Prepare mix for beef noodle dinner as directed on package except—substitute the diluted broth for the 3¼ cups hot water. Ten minutes before end of cooking time, stir in peas and pimiento.

4 or 5 servings.

HAMBURGER PIZZA

CRUST

2½ cups biscuit baking mix
1 package active dry yeast
⅔ cup hot water

MEAT MIXTURE

1 pound ground beef
1 medium onion, chopped (about ½ cup)
1 can (15 ounces) tomato sauce
2 teaspoons oregano leaves
¼ teaspoon pepper

TOPPING

½ cup chopped green pepper (optional)
2 cups shredded Cheddar or mozzarella cheese (8 ounces)
1 cup grated Parmesan cheese

Heat oven to 425°. Mix baking mix and yeast; stir in water and beat vigorously. Turn dough onto well-floured surface; knead until smooth, about 20 times. Let dough rest a few minutes.

While dough is resting, cook and stir meat and onion in large skillet until onion is tender. Drain off fat. Stir in tomato sauce, oregano leaves and pepper; set aside.

Divide dough in half. Roll each half on ungreased baking sheet into rectangle, 13×10 inches, or on pizza pan into 12-inch circle. Pinch edges to make a slight rim. Spread Meat Mixture almost to edges. Top with green pepper and cheeses. Bake until crust is brown and filling is hot and bubbly, 15 to 20 minutes. Cut into squares or wedges.

2 pizzas.

You can get a head start on this recipe with Beef-Tomato Freezer Mix (see page 66).

BAKED PIZZA SANDWICH

1 pound ground beef
1 can (15 ounces) tomato sauce or pizza sauce
1 teaspoon oregano leaves
2 cups biscuit baking mix
1 egg
⅔ cup milk
1 package (8 ounces) sliced process American or mozzarella cheese
1 can (2 ounces) sliced mushrooms, drained
¼ cup grated Parmesan cheese

Heat oven to 400°. Cook and stir meat in large skillet until brown. Drain off fat. Stir half the tomato sauce and the oregano leaves into meat; heat to boiling. Reduce heat and simmer uncovered 10 minutes.

While meat mixture is simmering, mix baking mix, egg and milk. Measure ¾ cup of the batter and set aside. Spread remaining batter in greased baking pan, 9×9×2 inches. Pour remaining tomato sauce over batter, spreading it evenly. Layer 4 slices cheese, the meat mixture, mushrooms and remaining cheese slices on batter. Spoon reserved batter on top. Sprinkle with Parmesan cheese. Bake uncovered until golden brown, 20 to 25 minutes. Cool 5 minutes, then cut into squares.

5 or 6 servings.

MINNESOTA MINESTRONE

- 2 pounds ground beef
- 1 large onion, chopped (about 1 cup)
- 1 clove garlic, minced
- 1 can (28 ounces) tomatoes
- 1 can (15 ounces) kidney beans
- 1 can (12 ounces) vacuum-pack whole kernel corn
- 2 stalks celery, sliced (about 1 cup)
- 2 cups shredded cabbage (about ¼ head)
- 2 small zucchini, sliced (about 2 cups)
- 1 cup uncooked elbow macaroni or broken spaghetti
- 2 cups water
- ½ cup red wine or water
- 2 teaspoons instant beef bouillon
- 1½ teaspoons salt
- 1½ teaspoons Italian seasoning
  Grated Parmesan cheese

Cook and stir meat, onion and garlic in Dutch oven until meat is brown. Drain off fat. Stir in tomatoes (with liquid), kidney beans (with liquid), corn (with liquid) and remaining ingredients except cheese; break up tomatoes.

Heat to boiling. Reduce heat; cover and simmer, stirring occasionally, until macaroni and vegetables are tender, about 30 minutes. Serve with Parmesan cheese. (Pictured on page 54.)

10 servings (1½ cups each).

WIPE AWAY THOSE TEARS!

If you're one of those cooks who start to weep at the very thought of chopping onions, take heart. Here's a new trick to try. Cut the ends off the onions, peel and rinse under cold water; then wrap and refrigerate for at least an hour or two. When ready to use, simply chop with a sharp knife.

BEEF AND LENTIL STEW

- 1 pound ground beef
- 1 medium onion, chopped (about ½ cup)
- 1 clove garlic, minced
- 1 can (4 ounces) mushroom stems and pieces
- 1 can (16 ounces) stewed tomatoes
- 1 stalk celery, sliced
- 1 large carrot, sliced
- 1 cup uncooked lentils
- 3 cups water
- ¼ cup red wine (optional)
- 1 bay leaf
- 2 tablespoons snipped parsley
- 2 teaspoons salt
- 1 teaspoon instant beef bouillon
- ¼ teaspoon pepper

Cook and stir meat, onion and garlic in Dutch oven until meat is brown. Drain off fat. Stir in mushrooms (with liquid) and remaining ingredients; heat to boiling. Reduce heat; cover and simmer, stirring occasionally, until lentils are tender, about 40 minutes. Remove bay leaf.

6 servings (1⅓ cups each).

Freezer Fare

To take full advantage of all that you're doing (or want to do), take full advantage of your freezer and of all the good foods that can be stored in it. Particularly hamburger. And that's what this chapter is all about. Here we show you how to make the most of the time you have—when you have it—with a special collection of hamburger recipes that will help you get a head start on the dinner hour.

Leading off, you will find a triple-threat attack on time with hamburger "freezer mixes," especially developed for savory spin-offs as sandwich, soup or casserole. And talk about variety. These mixes come in three very different flavor combinations:

BEEF-MUSHROOM FREEZER MIX—Browned beef with a delicate mushroom sauce, the easy beginning for cream-based dishes.

BROWNED 'N SEASONED FREEZER MIX—A combination of browned beef with onions and seasonings, frozen in a crumbly form that can be easily measured and used without thawing.

BEEF-TOMATO FREEZER MIX—Browned beef in a spicy tomato sauce, to start off any number of tangy tomato-based favorites.

Note, too, that we've included information for thawing *and* heating these mixes in the time-saving microwave oven.

Next, "Individual Dinners in Foil," some very special ideas for a family on the go. With these, you can make your dinner whenever the spirit strikes; then divvy it up in individual serving packets, label and freeze. These one-per-person dinner packets are sure to fit the comings and goings of today's life-styles. And they're perfect for double-quick heating in a microwave oven. (Timing tip: One or more packets can be heated in a conventional oven in the same amount of time. In a microwave oven, you must allow extra time for each extra packet.)

What about the all-time favorites? They're here too. "Favorite Fixin's" details the freezer treatment—including storage times and heating directions—for a number of recipes from other chapters. Take a tip and think about setting aside a few hours to "cook" for your freezer, and then relax in the knowledge that dinner will *always* be waiting, however busy the day.

Now stop and think about the way you use your freezer. Are you planning on it—and with it—to help free up your food time? We think it's the easy answer to how you can manage —in spite of, and because of, all you do in your busy days.

Beef-Mushroom Freezer Mix

4 pounds ground beef
2½ large onions, chopped (about 2½ cups)
2 cloves garlic, minced
3 cans (10¾ ounces each) condensed
   cream of mushroom soup
3 cans (4 ounces each) mushroom stems
   and pieces, drained
½ cup water or red wine
1 tablespoon instant beef bouillon
½ teaspoon pepper

Cook and stir meat in Dutch oven until brown. Drain off fat. Stir in remaining ingredients; heat to boiling. Reduce heat; cover and simmer 15 minutes, stirring occasionally. Divide mixture among four 1-quart freezer containers (about 3 cups in each). Cool quickly. Cover and label; freeze no longer than 3 months (see note). Use freezer mix in the recipes that follow.

About 12 cups.

NOTE: Mixture can be stored in refrigerator up to 3 days. When using in these recipes, add water and other ingredients as directed but decrease cooking time.

FREEZER MIX
MEAT-AND-POTATO FAVORITE

1 container frozen Beef-Mushroom
   Freezer Mix
⅓ cup water
2 cups frozen fried shredded potato rounds

Dip container of frozen mix into hot water just to loosen. In 2-quart saucepan, heat frozen mix and water to boiling. Reduce heat; cover and simmer, stirring frequently, until mix is thawed, about 20 minutes.

Heat oven to 375°. Place half the potato rounds in ungreased 1½-quart casserole; pour meat mixture over potato rounds and top with remaining potato rounds. Cover and bake 25 minutes. Uncover and bake until potato rounds are brown, about 10 minutes longer.

4 servings.

MICROWAVE COOKING TIPS

To defrost and heat frozen mixture in microwave oven, place freezer container in microwave oven and cook 4 minutes just to loosen. Place frozen mix in 2-quart casserole; omit water but make any other ingredient additions as directed in the recipes that follow. Cover and cook in microwave oven, stirring occasionally, until hot, 12 to 15 minutes. Add any remaining ingredients as directed and cook in microwave oven until of desired doneness, 5 to 15 minutes. (The time will depend on the amount of added ingredients and whether the ingredients are just being heated or actually being cooked.)

FREEZER MIX CHILIES CASSEROLE

1 container frozen Beef-Mushroom
  Freezer Mix
¼ cup water
1 can (10 ounces) mild or hot enchilada
  sauce
1 can (4 ounces) green chilies
1 can (4 ounces) red chilies (see note)
3 cups corn chips
1½ cups shredded Cheddar cheese

Dip container of frozen mix into hot water just to loosen. In 2-quart saucepan, heat frozen mix, water and enchilada sauce to boiling. Reduce heat; cover and simmer, stirring frequently, until mix is thawed, about 20 minutes.

Heat oven to 350°. Rinse green and red chilies to remove seeds (the seeds are very hot). Cut chilies into small pieces. Arrange 2 cups of the corn chips and half each of the meat mixture, chilies and cheese in ungreased baking dish, 10 × 6 × 1¾ inches; repeat with remaining meat mixture, chilies and cheese. Sprinkle with remaining corn chips. Bake uncovered until casserole is bubbly, 30 to 35 minutes.

4 or 5 servings.

NOTE: This casserole is hot and spicy. If you prefer a milder flavor, you can substitute 1 can (2 ounces) sliced pimiento, drained, for the red chilies.

FREEZER MIX STROGANOFF

1 container frozen Beef-Mushroom
  Freezer Mix
¼ cup water
¾ cup dairy sour cream
2 cups hot cooked noodles or rice

Dip container of frozen mix into hot water just to loosen. In 2-quart saucepan, heat frozen mix and water to boiling. Reduce heat; cover and simmer, stirring frequently, until mix is thawed, about 20 minutes. Stir in sour cream and heat. Serve over noodles.

4 servings.

FREEZER MIX CHOW MEIN

1 container frozen Beef-Mushroom
   Freezer Mix
¼ cup water
1 tablespoon soy sauce
2 teaspoons cornstarch
2 teaspoons molasses
¼ teaspoon ginger
1 can (16 ounces) Chinese vegetables,
   drained
2 to 3 cups chow mein noodles or
   hot cooked rice

Dip container of frozen mix into hot water just to loosen. In 2-quart saucepan, heat frozen mix and water to boiling. Reduce heat; cover and simmer, stirring frequently, until mix is thawed, about 20 minutes.

Mix soy sauce, cornstarch, molasses and ginger; stir soy sauce mixture and Chinese vegetables into meat mixture. Cook, stirring constantly, until mixture thickens and boils. Boil and stir 1 minute. Serve over chow mein noodles and top with additional soy sauce.

4 servings.

FREEZER MIX BARLEY SOUP

1 container frozen Beef-Mushroom
   Freezer Mix
3 cups water
½ cup uncooked barley
1 cup sliced celery
1 cup sliced carrot
1 sprig parsley
1 bay leaf
¾ teaspoon salt

Dip container of frozen mix into hot water just to loosen. In Dutch oven, heat frozen mix and remaining ingredients to boiling. Reduce heat; cover and simmer, stirring frequently, until mix is thawed and barley and vegetables are tender, 30 to 40 minutes. Remove bay leaf.

4 servings (1½ cups each).

FREEZER MIX ROMANOFF

1 container frozen Beef-Mushroom
   Freezer Mix
⅓ cup water
1 package (5.5 ounces) noodles Romanoff

Dip container of frozen mix into hot water just to loosen. In 2-quart saucepan, heat frozen mix and water to boiling. Reduce heat; cover and simmer, stirring frequently, until mix is thawed, about 20 minutes.

Prepare noodles Romanoff as directed on package except—omit butter and milk; stir sour cream–cheese sauce mix and cooked noodles into meat mixture and heat to boiling. Reduce heat; cover and simmer 5 minutes.

4 or 5 servings.

Browned 'n Seasoned Freezer Mix

4 pounds ground beef
1½ large onions, chopped (about 1½ cups)
3 cloves garlic, minced
2 teaspoons salt
¾ teaspoon pepper

Cook and stir meat, onions and garlic in Dutch oven until meat is brown. Drain off fat. Stir in seasonings. Spread meat mixture in 2 ungreased baking pans, 13×9×2 inches. Freeze 1 hour. (This partial freezing prevents the meat from freezing together solidly.)

Crumble meat mixture into small pieces; place in heavy plastic bag or freezer container. Seal securely and label; freeze no longer than 3 months. Use freezer mix in the recipes that follow.

About 14 cups.

NOTE: You can use this mix in any recipe for drained, seasoned browned ground beef. Each 3½ cups lightly packed frozen mix is the equivalent of 1 pound ground beef, ⅓ cup chopped onion, 1 small clove garlic, ½ teaspoon salt and dash of pepper. (If mixture is not frozen, allow 3 cups.)

FREEZER MIX DINNER

Prepare 1 package (7 ounces) mix for beef noodle dinner or 1 package (8 ounces) mix for chili tomato dinner as directed except—substitute 3½ cups lightly packed frozen Browned 'n Seasoned Freezer Mix for the drained browned ground beef.

5 servings (1 cup each).

FREEZER MIX
MEAT AND POTATOES AU GRATIN

Prepare 1 package (5.5 ounces) au gratin potatoes as directed except—use 2-quart casserole, omit butter and stir in 3½ cups lightly packed frozen Browned 'n Seasoned Freezer Mix with the water.

4 or 5 servings.

FREEZER MIX SKILLET GOULASH

Prepare Skillet Goulash (page 36) except—substitute 3½ cups lightly packed frozen Browned 'n Seasoned Freezer Mix for the drained browned ground beef and onion; decrease salt to 1 teaspoon.

5 servings (1 cup each).

FREEZER MIX ALL-AMERICAN HOT DISH

Prepare All-American Hot Dish (page 37) except—substitute 3½ cups lightly packed frozen Browned 'n Seasoned Freezer Mix for the drained browned ground beef and onion; omit salt.

6 servings (1 cup each).

FREEZER MIX BEEF-NOODLE COMBO

Prepare Creamy Beef-Noodle Combo (page 37) except—substitute 3½ cups lightly packed frozen Browned 'n Seasoned Freezer Mix for the drained browned ground beef and onion; decrease salt to ½ teaspoon.

5 servings (1 cup each).

FREEZER MIX CHEESEBURGER PIE

Prepare Cheeseburger Pie (page 48) except—substitute 3½ cups lightly packed frozen Browned 'n Seasoned Freezer Mix, 2 tablespoons biscuit baking mix and 1 tablespoon Worcestershire sauce for the Meat Filling. (Pictured on page 52.)

6 servings.

FREEZER MIX PASTIES

Prepare Hamburger Pasties (page 17) except—substitute 3½ cups lightly packed frozen Browned 'n Seasoned Freezer Mix for the drained browned ground beef and onion; omit garlic salt and pepper.

8 pasties.

FREEZER MIX PIZZAWICHES

1 can (6 ounces) tomato paste
¼ cup grated Parmesan cheese
3½ cups lightly packed frozen Browned
  'n Seasoned Freezer Mix
1 teaspoon Italian seasoning
  Dash red pepper sauce
6 slices bread or 5 hamburger buns, split
  Shredded mozzarella or process American
  cheese

Heat oven to 500°. Mix tomato paste, Parmesan cheese, freezer mix and seasonings. Spread mixture on bread slices and place on ungreased baking sheet. Top each with a spoonful of shredded cheese. Bake until cheese is bubbly, 5 to 10 minutes. (Pictured on page 52.)

5 or 6 servings.

Beef-Tomato Freezer Mix

4 pounds ground beef
2½ large onions, chopped (about 2½ cups)
1 cup chopped green pepper
3 cloves garlic, minced
3 cans (15 ounces each) tomato sauce
1 can (12 ounces) tomato paste
2 teaspoons salt
¾ teaspoon pepper

Cook and stir meat in Dutch oven until brown. Drain off fat. Stir in remaining ingredients; heat to boiling. Reduce heat; cover and simmer 15 minutes, stirring occasionally. Divide mixture among four 1-quart freezer containers (about 3 cups in each). Cool quickly. Cover and label; freeze no longer than 3 months (see note). Use freezer mix in the recipes that follow.

About 12 cups.

NOTE: If you prefer, the mixture can be stored in the refrigerator up to 3 days. When using in the following recipes, add water and other ingredients as directed but decrease the cooking time.

FREEZER MIX GOULASH

1 container frozen Beef-Tomato Freezer Mix
¼ cup water
¼ cup catsup
1 cup sliced celery
1 can (4 ounces) mushroom stems and pieces, drained
1 teaspoon paprika
1 teaspoon brown sugar
1 teaspoon Worcestershire sauce
3 ounces noodles (about 1½ cups)

Dip container of frozen mix into hot water just to loosen. Place frozen mix and remaining ingredients except noodles in 2-quart saucepan; heat to boiling. Reduce heat; cover and simmer, stirring frequently, until mix is thawed and celery is tender, about 40 minutes.

While meat mixture is simmering, cook noodles as directed on package; drain. Stir noodles into meat mixture and simmer until hot.

4 servings.

MICROWAVE COOKING TIPS

To defrost and heat frozen mixture in microwave oven, place freezer container in microwave oven and cook 4 minutes just to loosen. Place frozen mix in 2-quart casserole; omit water but make any other ingredient additions as directed in the recipes that follow. Cover and cook in microwave oven, stirring occasionally, until hot, 12 to 15 minutes. Add any remaining ingredients as directed and cook in microwave oven until of desired doneness, 5 to 15 minutes. (The time will depend on the amount of added ingredients and whether the ingredients are just being heated or actually being cooked.)

FREEZER MIX SPANISH RICE

- 1 container frozen Beef-Tomato Freezer Mix
- 5 slices bacon, crisply fried and crumbled
- 1 cup uncooked regular rice
- 2½ cups water
- 1 teaspoon chili powder
- ½ teaspoon oregano leaves

Dip container of frozen mix into hot water just to loosen. In large skillet, heat frozen mix and remaining ingredients to boiling. Reduce heat; cover and simmer, stirring occasionally, until mix is thawed and rice is tender, about 30 minutes. (A small amount of water can be added if necessary.)

4 servings (1 cup each).

FREEZER MIX MEXICAN CASSEROLE

- 1 container frozen Beef-Tomato Freezer Mix
- 1½ to 2 teaspoons chili powder
- ⅓ cup water
- 1 can (16 ounces) whole kernel corn, drained
- 1 can (2¼ ounces) sliced ripe olives, drained (½ cup)
- ½ cup biscuit baking mix
- ¼ cup yellow cornmeal
- ¾ cup shredded Cheddar cheese
- 1 egg
- 3 tablespoons milk

Dip container of frozen mix into hot water just to loosen. In 2-quart saucepan, heat frozen mix, chili powder and water to boiling. Reduce heat; cover and simmer, stirring frequently, until mix is partially thawed, about 15 minutes. Stir in corn and olives; heat to boiling. Reduce heat; cover and simmer 5 minutes.

Heat oven to 400°. While meat mixture is simmering, mix remaining ingredients. Pour hot meat mixture into ungreased 2-quart casserole. Drop batter by teaspoonfuls about ½ inch apart onto meat mixture. (The batter will bake together to form crust.) Bake uncovered 20 minutes.

4 or 5 servings.

FREEZER MIX ENCHILADA CASSEROLE

1 container frozen Beef-Tomato
   Freezer Mix
¼ cup water
1 can (2¼ ounces) sliced ripe olives,
   drained (½ cup)
1½ to 2 teaspoons chili powder
6 corn tortillas
1½ cups shredded Cheddar or Monterey
   Jack cheese

Dip container of frozen mix into hot water just to loosen. In 2-quart saucepan, heat frozen mix, water, olives and chili powder to boiling. Reduce heat; cover and simmer, stirring frequently, until mix is thawed, about 20 minutes.

Heat oven to 375°. Layer half each of the tortillas, meat mixture and cheese in ungreased baking dish, 11¾ × 7½ × 1¾ inches; repeat. Bake uncovered until bubbly, 30 to 40 minutes.

4 or 5 servings.

FREEZER MIX LASAGNE

Prepare Lasagne (page 38) except—substitute the following mixture for the Meat Sauce:

1 container frozen Beef-Tomato Freezer Mix
½ teaspoon oregano leaves
1 tablespoon snipped parsley
¼ cup water

Dip container of frozen mix into hot water just to loosen. In 2-quart saucepan, heat frozen mix, oregano leaves, parsley and water to boiling. Reduce heat; cover and simmer 15 minutes, stirring frequently. Uncover and simmer, stirring occasionally, until mix is thawed.

6 servings.

FREEZER MIX PIZZA

Prepare Hamburger Pizza (page 56) except—omit green pepper in Topping and substitute the following mixture for the Meat Mixture:

1 container frozen Beef-Tomato Freezer Mix
¼ cup water
1 teaspoon Italian seasoning
   Dash red pepper sauce

Dip container of frozen mix into hot water just to loosen. In 2-quart saucepan, heat frozen mix and remaining ingredients to boiling. Reduce heat; cover and simmer, stirring frequently, until mix is thawed, about 20 minutes.

2 pizzas.

FREEZER MIX ONE-DISH SPAGHETTI

1 container frozen Beef-Tomato Freezer Mix
3 cups water
1 can (4 ounces) mushroom stems and
   pieces, drained
1 package (7 ounces) thin spaghetti,
   broken into pieces
1 teaspoon oregano leaves
1 teaspoon sugar
1 teaspoon chili powder
1 cup shredded Cheddar cheese (4 ounces)

Dip container of frozen mix into hot water just to loosen. In Dutch oven, heat frozen mix and remaining ingredients except cheese to boiling. Reduce heat; cover and simmer, stirring frequently, until mix is thawed and spaghetti is tender, about 30 minutes. (A small amount of water can be added if necessary.) Sprinkle with cheese; cover and heat until cheese is melted. (Pictured on page 53.)

6 servings (1 cup each).

EASY FREEZER MIX STIR-INS

Dip 1 container frozen Beef-Tomato Freezer Mix into hot water just to loosen. In 2-quart saucepan, heat frozen mix and ¼ cup water to boiling. Reduce heat; cover and simmer, stirring frequently, until mix is thawed, about 20 minutes.

Stir in 1 or 2 cans (15 ounces each) spaghetti in tomato and cheese sauce or 1 or 2 cans (14¾ ounces each) macaroni and cheese; heat to boiling. Reduce heat; simmer uncovered 5 minutes.

4 to 6 servings.

FREEZER MIX LENTIL STEW

    1 container frozen Beef-Tomato
      Freezer Mix
    3 cups water
    1 cup uncooked lentils
    1 sprig parsley
    1 bay leaf
 1½ cups sliced fresh mushrooms (optional)
    1 large carrot, sliced
    1 large stalk celery, sliced
    ¼ cup red wine (optional)
    ½ teaspoon salt

Dip container of frozen mix into hot water just to loosen. In Dutch oven, heat frozen mix, water, lentils, parsley and bay leaf to boiling. Reduce heat; cover and simmer, stirring frequently, until mix is thawed, about 20 minutes.

Stir in remaining ingredients; heat to boiling. Reduce heat; cover and simmer until vegetables are tender, about 20 minutes. Remove bay leaf. (Pictured on page 53.)

5 servings (1⅓ cups each).

FREEZER MIX SLOPPY JOES

    1 container frozen Beef-Tomato Freezer Mix
    ¼ cup water
    1 cup sliced celery
    1 tablespoon catsup
    1 teaspoon brown sugar (optional)
    1 teaspoon Worcestershire sauce
 6 to 8 hamburger buns, split and toasted

Dip container of frozen mix into hot water just to loosen. In 2-quart saucepan, heat frozen mix, water, celery, catsup, brown sugar and Worcestershire sauce to boiling. Reduce heat; cover and simmer, stirring frequently, until mix is partially thawed, about 15 minutes. Uncover and simmer, stirring occasionally, until of desired consistency, about 10 minutes. Spoon onto bottom halves of buns; top with remaining halves.

6 to 8 sandwiches.

FREEZER MIX TACOS

Prepare Tacos (page 17) except—substitute the following mixture for the Meat Filling:

    1 container frozen Beef-Tomato Freezer Mix
    1 to 2 teaspoons chili powder
    ⅛ teaspoon cayenne red pepper (optional)
      Dash red pepper sauce
    ¼ cup water

Dip container of frozen mix into hot water just to loosen. In 2-quart saucepan, heat frozen mix and remaining ingredients to boiling. Reduce heat; cover and simmer, stirring frequently, until mix is partially thawed, about 15 minutes. Uncover and simmer 15 minutes, stirring occasionally.

8 to 10 tacos.

Individual Dinners in Foil

Here's a handy treatment to fit any family's catch-as-catch-can dinner schedule.

Cooking Guide for Individual Foil Dinners

TO SERVE FROM REGULAR OVEN: Place the desired number of frozen packets seam sides up on ungreased baking sheet. Bake on center rack of 450° oven until hot, 35 to 45 minutes.

TO SERVE FROM MICROWAVE OVEN: Unwrap *one* packet and place in a small glass dish; cover with dinner plate. Cook, stirring once, until hot, 5 to 7 minutes. (Each serving can also be packaged and stored in paper or glass dishes or in plastic cooking bags, enabling it to go *directly* from freezer to microwave oven. Do not unwrap.)

INDIVIDUAL SAUCY MEAT PATTIES IN FOIL

2 pounds ground beef
1 envelope (about 1½ ounces) onion
  soup mix
1 can (10¾ ounces) condensed cream of
  mushroom soup

Mix meat and onion soup mix. Shape mixture into 8 patties, about ¾ inch thick. Place each patty on 12-inch square of heavy-duty or double thickness regular aluminum foil. Spoon about 2½ tablespoons soup onto each patty. Wrap each securely and label; freeze no longer than 3 months.

When ready to serve, cook according to Cooking Guide (above) except—if using microwave oven, cover with waxed paper instead of dinner plate.

8 patties.

INDIVIDUAL BEEF-AND-BEAN DINNERS

1 pound ground beef
1 small onion, chopped (about ¼ cup)
2 cans (16 ounces each) pork and beans
  in tomato sauce
⅓ cup chili sauce
1 tablespoon molasses or brown sugar
1 tablespoon prepared mustard
½ teaspoon salt

Cook and stir meat and onion in large skillet until onion is tender. Drain off fat. Remove from heat; stir in remaining ingredients. Divide mixture among five 12-inch squares of heavy-duty or double thickness regular aluminum foil. Wrap each securely and label; freeze no longer than 2 months.

When ready to serve, cook according to Cooking Guide (above).

5 servings.

INDIVIDUAL MEAT-MACARONI DINNERS

1 pound ground beef
1 small onion, chopped (about ¼ cup)
1 cup elbow macaroni, cooked and
   drained
1 can (11 ounces) condensed Cheddar
   cheese soup
1 can (16 ounces) mixed vegetables,
   drained
⅓ cup water
¼ teaspoon pepper

Cook and stir meat and onion in large skillet until onion is tender. Drain off fat. Remove from heat; stir in remaining ingredients. Divide mixture among four 12-inch squares of heavy-duty or double thickness regular aluminum foil. Wrap each securely and label; freeze no longer than 2 months.

When ready to serve, cook according to Cooking Guide (page 68).

4 servings.

INDIVIDUAL SOUPER BEEF DINNERS

1 pound ground beef
1 small onion, chopped (about ¼ cup)
1 can (10¾ ounces) condensed cream
   of mushroom soup
1 can (16 ounces) cut green beans or
   whole kernel corn, drained
¼ cup water
1 can (3½ ounces) French fried onions

Cook and stir meat and onion in large skillet until onion is tender. Drain off fat. Remove from heat; stir in remaining ingredients except French fried onions. Divide mixture among four 12-inch squares of heavy-duty or double thickness regular aluminum foil. Wrap each securely and label; freeze no longer than 2 months.

When ready to serve, cook according to Cooking Guide (page 68) except—open packets during the last 5 minutes of baking and sprinkle with French fried onions. If using microwave oven, sprinkle with onions after cooking.

4 servings.

INDIVIDUAL TOMATO-RICE DINNERS

1 pound ground beef
1 small onion, chopped (about ¼ cup)
1 can (10¾ ounces) condensed tomato
   soup
1½ cups uncooked instant rice
1 cup water
1 cup shredded Cheddar cheese
   (4 ounces)
½ cup chopped green pepper (optional)
½ teaspoon salt
½ teaspoon chili powder
¼ teaspoon teaspoon basil leaves
⅛ teaspoon pepper

Cook and stir meat and onion in large skillet until onion is tender. Drain off fat. Remove from heat; stir in remaining ingredients. Divide mixture among five 12-inch squares of heavy-duty or double thickness regular aluminum foil. Wrap each securely and label; freeze no longer than 2 months.

When ready to serve, cook according to Cooking Guide (page 68).

5 servings.

Favorite Fixin's

A main dish waiting in the freezer. It's the answer to a busy cook's prayers—with a little help from the preplanning department. On these two pages you'll find a variety of hamburger recipes from the previous chapters, here for do-ahead fixing and no-fuss cooking. You can also use them as a guide for handling your own hamburger favorites. But if you do, here are a couple of tips to keep in mind:

☐ Be sure to avoid overcooking—it's the major pitfall of casseroles destined for the freezer. (A simple way out is to always undercook any pasta or rice; it will cook through when the casserole is reheated.) It's a good idea to soft-pedal spices too.

☐ Reheat frozen cooked casseroles in a 350° oven (usually 1 to 1½ hours), adding liquid if the food seems dry. Or empty the frozen dish into a saucepan (with a small amount of butter, margarine or water in the pan), cover tightly and place over medium heat.

FREEZER BURGERS

Prepare Basic Hamburgers (page 6) except—do not cook. Wrap each securely in heavy-duty or double thickness regular aluminum foil and label; freeze no longer than 3 months.

TO COOK IN SKILLET: Unwrap desired number of frozen patties and place in single layer in skillet. Cover and cook over medium-high heat 5 to 7 minutes. Turn patties; partially cover and cook over medium heat until of desired doneness, 5 to 7 minutes.

TO BROIL: Unwrap desired number of frozen patties and place on rack in broiler pan. Broil patties 6 inches from heat, turning once, to desired doneness, about 20 minutes.

6 patties.

FREEZER MEAT LOAF

Prepare Basic Meat Loaf (page 30) except—do not bake. Cover pan with aluminum foil and label; freeze no longer than 2 months.

TO SERVE: Bake frozen meat loaf uncovered in 350° oven 2 to 2¼ hours. Drain off fat.

6 servings.

FREEZER LASAGNE

Prepare Lasagne (page 38) except—do not bake. Cover with aluminum foil and label; freeze no longer than 2 months.

TO SERVE: Bake foil-covered frozen Lasagne in 350° oven 1¼ hours. Uncover and bake until golden brown, 15 to 30 minutes longer.

6 servings.

FREEZER MEATBALLS

Meatballs can be frozen either before or after cooking. Prepare Basic Meatballs (page 18) except—after shaping or cooking, place in ungreased shallow baking pan and freeze uncovered 3 hours. (This prevents the meatballs from freezing together.) Remove from freezer and pack desired number of meatballs in heavy plastic bags or freezer containers or wrap in heavy-duty or double thickness regular aluminum foil; label. Freeze no longer than 3 months.

TO COOK FROZEN UNCOOKED MEATBALLS: Cook frozen meatballs in skillet or oven as directed in basic recipe except—increase baking time to 25 minutes.

TO REHEAT FROZEN COOKED MEATBALLS: Place frozen meatballs in ungreased baking pan and heat in 375° oven until hot, about 20 minutes. Or add frozen cooked meatballs to a sauce and simmer until hot, about 15 minutes.

About 24 meatballs.

FREEZER PASTIES

Prepare Hamburger Pasties (page 17) except— do not prick tops or bake. Wrap each pasty securely in heavy-duty or double thickness regular aluminum foil and label; freeze no longer than 2 months.

TO SERVE: Unwrap desired number of frozen pasties and place on ungreased baking sheet. Prick tops with fork and bake in 375° oven until hot, 40 to 45 minutes.

8 pasties.

FREEZER ENCHILADAS

Prepare Enchiladas (page 41) except—place filled tortillas in ungreased baking pan, 13 × 9 × 2 inches; do not bake. Cover pan with aluminum foil and label; freeze no longer than 2 months.

TO SERVE: Pour ⅓ cup water over frozen Enchiladas; cover and bake in 350° oven 1 hour. Uncover and bake until golden brown and bubbly, about 15 minutes longer.

4 or 5 servings.

FREEZER MANICOTTI

Prepare Manicotti (page 40) except—after filling shells, wrap securely in heavy-duty or double thickness or regular aluminum foil and label; freeze no longer than 2 months. Do not prepare Tomato Sauce.

TO SERVE: Unwrap frozen shells and place in ungreased baking pan, 13 × 9 × 2 inches. Prepare Tomato Sauce and pour over shells. Cover and bake until shells are tender, 1¾ to 2 hours.

6 to 8 servings.

FREEZER STUFFED GREEN PEPPERS

Prepare Stuffed Green Peppers (page 45) except —stir all the tomato sauce into the filling mixture; cover with aluminum foil but do not bake. Label; freeze no longer than 2 months.

TO SERVE: Bake foil-covered pan of frozen peppers in 350° oven until hot, 1 to 1¼ hours. Uncover; top peppers with Cheddar cheese slices, catsup or chili sauce and bake 5 minutes.

4 or 5 servings.

Microwave Specials

If you're the proud possessor of a microwave oven, you've no doubt discovered how its speed in cooking has added to the flexibility of your mealtime. But have you used it for your hamburger favorites? If not, you really ought to give it a try.

On the following pages we bring you some basic recipes that appear in other sections of the book, this time adapted to microwave cooking. And although we have included only a sampling, the principles can be applied to many other hamburger-based recipes.

Notice, for example, that when meatballs are not accompanied by a sauce or gravy, we have suggested coating them with gravy mix to produce the appetizing brown color and flavor you're accustomed to.

Observe that we recommend shaping meat loaf in a shallower than usual form so that quick cooking will also mean even cooking.

If a hamburger casserole is the order of the day, the meat is first partially cooked in the microwave oven so that the fat can be drained off before any other ingredients are added.

Finally, when the recipe calls for covered cooking but your casserole lacks a fitting cover, you can try waxed paper or a dinner plate instead.

To help you make the most of your valuable time, we've applied the double-quick microwave method to some of the done-in-advance fare that you've stored in the freezer. All of the "freezer mixes" (see pages 59–67) can be defrosted *and* heated in a microwave oven, while an "individual dinner in foil" (see pages 68–69) can be taken from the freezer, popped into the microwave oven and ready to serve in less than 10 minutes.

Of course, there are certain variations in the performance of individual microwave ovens— just as there are in conventional ovens. The recipes in this chapter were tested in counter-top microwave ovens that plug into regular grounded 110- or 120-volt outlets, and a range of cooking times has been indicated to allow for individual differences in oven cooking patterns. Start with the minimum time and then increase the time if necessary to achieve the "doneness" described in the recipe. (For other types of microwave ovens, refer to the manufacturer's instruction book.)

Using these recipes as a starting point, you can perfect your technique of cooking a wide variety of hamburger dishes in your microwave oven. Success with these should encourage you to go on and adapt your own favorites.

MEAT LOAF IN A MICROWAVE OVEN

Prepare Basic Meat Loaf (page 30) except—spread mixture in ungreased 10-inch glass pie pan and spoon catsup on top. Cover with inverted glass pie pan or dinner plate and cook in microwave oven until meat is set in center, 18 to 20 minutes. Let stand covered 5 minutes before serving.

6 servings.

NOTE: The meat loaf cooks faster and more evenly in a shallow round shape, rather like a pie, than in the traditional loaf shape.

BROWNED MEATBALLS
IN A MICROWAVE OVEN

Prepare Basic Meatballs (page 18) except—coat meatballs with 1 envelope (about 1 ounce) brown gravy mix and arrange in ungreased glass baking dish, 8×8×2 inches. Cover with waxed paper and cook in microwave oven until done, 7 to 8 minutes. Drain off fat.

About 24 meatballs.

NOTE: The gravy mix adds a brown color and flavor similar to that achieved by conventional browning.

SAUCY MEATBALLS
IN A MICROWAVE OVEN

Basic Meatballs (page 18)
1 can (10¾ ounces) condensed cream of chicken soup
⅓ cup milk
⅛ teaspoon nutmeg
½ cup dairy sour cream
Snipped parsley

Prepare Basic Meatballs except—place meatballs in ungreased glass baking dish, 8×8×2 inches. Cover with waxed paper and cook in microwave oven 5 to 6 minutes. Drain off fat.

Stir in soup, milk and nutmeg. Cover with waxed paper and cook in microwave oven until mixture is bubbly, about 5 minutes. Stir in sour cream and cook in microwave oven 1 minute. Garnish with parsley.

4 or 5 servings.

NOTE: When the meatballs are served in a sauce, as is the case in this recipe, the gravy mix coating is not necessary because the sauce provides all the color and flavor needed.

GIVE IT A TURN

If the manufacturer of your microwave oven recommends that you turn the cooking container once or twice during the cooking period, follow the same procedure with your own hamburger favorites. And this is especially true for a dish that doesn't call for stirring or turning over. An occasional quarter-turn will assure even cooking.

BEEF AND CABBAGE JOES
IN A MICROWAVE OVEN

1 pound ground beef
1 medium onion, chopped (about ½ cup)
½ cup thinly sliced celery
2 cups shredded cabbage
⅓ cup chopped green pepper
¾ cup catsup
¼ teaspoon salt
1 tablespoon prepared mustard
8 hamburger buns, split and toasted

Crumble meat into ungreased 2-quart glass casserole; add onion and celery. Cook uncovered in microwave oven, stirring once, until meat is set, about 5 minutes. Drain off fat. Stir in remaining ingredients except buns. Cover and cook, stirring occasionally, until cabbage is desired doneness, about 14 minutes. Spoon onto bottom halves of buns; top with remaining halves.

8 sandwiches.

NOTE: By precooking the meat in the microwave oven before adding the sauce ingredients, it is possible to drain off the fat and keep the meat in small chunks, similar to those in conventional browning. When the precooking is omitted, the meat pieces will be very fine and the fat may need to be skimmed from the finished casserole.

CREAMY BEEF-NOODLE COMBO
IN A MICROWAVE OVEN

1 pound ground beef
1 medium onion, chopped (about ½ cup)
1 cup sliced celery
1 can (4 ounces) mushroom stems and
   pieces
1 can (10¾ ounces) condensed cream of
   mushroom soup
½ cup chopped green pepper
¼ cup sliced pimiento
1 cup milk
1 tablespoon Worcestershire sauce
1 teaspoon salt
4 ounces uncooked noodles (about 2 cups)

Crumble meat into ungreased 2- to 2½-quart glass casserole; add onion and celery. Cook uncovered in microwave oven, stirring once, until meat is set, about 5 minutes. Drain off fat. Stir in mushrooms (with liquid) and remaining ingredients; cover and cook, stirring occasionally, until noodles are tender, 15 to 20 minutes.

5 servings (1 cup each).

NOTE: The cooking time for this casserole is similar to the time required in a conventional oven because the noodles need the time to rehydrate.

Index